# TOWARD THE
# LIGHT

# TOWARD THE LIGHT

## RESCUING SPIRITS, TRAPPED SOULS, AND EARTHBOUND GHOSTS

## By Amy Major

NEW PAGE BOOKS
A division of The Career Press, Inc.
Pompton Plains, NJ

TOWARD THE LIGHT
EDITED BY ROGER SHEETY
Original cover design by Howard Grossman
Printed in the U.S.A.

To order this title, please call toll-free 1-800-CAREER-1 (NJ and Canada: 201-848-0310) to order using VISA or MasterCard, or for further information on books from Career Press.

The Career Press, Inc.
220 West Parkway, Unit 12
Pompton Plains, NJ 07444
**www.careerpress.com**
**www.newpagebooks.com**

Library of Congress Cataloging-in-Publication Data
Major, Amy, 1976-
    Toward the light : rescuing spirits, trapped souls, and earthbound ghosts / by Amy Major. -- 1 [edition].
        pages cm
    Includes index.
    ISBN 978-1-63265-000-9 -- ISBN 978-1-63265-999-6 (ebook)
        1. Spiritualism. I. Title.

BF1261.2.M327 2015
133.9'1--dc23
                                                            2015002856

To my family and Victoria Ladd, my partner in crime
and the best friend I've ever had.

# Contents

# INTRODUCTION
# A Little About Me

mediumship, psychic, and healing abilities. During this process, I had several negative experiences with spirits as well as positive ones, some of which I describe in this book. All of the experiences were to shape who I would become. Through the help from my guides, angels, and animal spirits, I learned how to develop my unique ability to aid those who were in need of help. I now devote my time to helping spirits cross over and educating people about spirit rescue.

# 1
# Connections

When we're born into our current lives, we're given tools and resources to help us learn lessons from our experiences to improve ourselves and aid in our soul's progression. Our life exists for a reason. We are here for a reason. Whether it's to help out a friend, balance out past life karma, fix mistakes, explore the world, or just lend a helping hand, we're all here to serve a purpose. Life isn't by chance, it's a choice—a choice made by you. In this choice, we choose helpers, friends, guides, and mates to help us in our journey of life.

This journey wasn't chosen by mistake. Everything that we encounter in our lives we decided upon before our birth. The people we meet, the challenges we face, and the experiences we encounter are all part of the big plan we decided upon before we arrived. With each life that we live, we strengthen our understanding of our connection to the Divine. Each life is a stepping stone on our path.

So if we chose this life before we came in, does this mean we've lived before? Absolutely. Reincarnation is the soul's continual progression through life cycles of death and rebirth. After each death, we can evaluate the life we just experienced to decide upon the next course of action in our next life. It's sort of like graduating to the next grade in school. Every time we complete a life that changes our soul's progress through a greater understanding of our spirit and its connection to the Divine, we pass to another grade level. With each grade level we encounter, the challenges become harder and lives can become harder as well. It's like getting more books, lessons, and homework with each higher grade. Sometimes these grades can take a long time to get through. It may take hundreds of lives to pass one grade, depending on how we live our lives and the choices we make.

Various accounts of past life regression have been documented. Some cases use hypnosis to bring back past life memories, while other cases are more direct, such as young children recalling detailed past lives. Most people find the challenges they face in their current life directly relate to the challenges of their past lives. This shows that what we bring in with us are continual lessons that our soul has yet to learn. Because of this, we choose friends, family, loved ones, and guides to help us make better choices in our lives to overcome these challenges. Each life is different and, therefore, each life will bring forth new ways to examine our soul's challenges and progression.

Some people choose to come into our lives only for a moment, whereas others stick around quite a long time. It all depends on what the purpose of the life is. Each life shares a new perspective of ourselves. You can relate it to the experiences you face in your life. With each chapter in your life that you face, you get a greater understanding of who you are and what your purpose is. The same rules apply for your soul and the various lives we live. Each life makes us understand ourselves a little more through various perspectives and experiences. So, in turn, each life will have a different purpose depending on what you're trying to learn and understand about yourself. Some souls may have progressed enough through the grades that their life purpose is to educate and help others. These souls may come in as teachers, guides, counselors, spiritual mentors, or religious figures. All will feel the need in their own way to help nurture and support those around them.

The reality is it's sometimes hard to know the purpose of your life. Life's issues and personal fears get in the way from truly seeing our life purpose. Because of this, we are helped

her. She might enjoy nocturnal activities and like working late night shifts.

Though it's not essential that you connect to your power animal, it is recommended. Connecting to your animal spirits may provide a greater spiritual understanding of yourself and your life purpose. Power animals have subtle ways to show themselves to you. For example, do you feel drawn to a certain animal? Do you find specific animals are always in your life? Do you feel you take on the same traits or personalities of certain animals? These are all hints to your power animal.

We also have message animals that come into our life temporarily like lesson guides. Message animals show up to be of service when we need a little more assistance. These animals bring us messages to let us know when we should be aware of something, encourage us to complete something, help us through times of change, or provide messages of hope and inspiration. Each message animal has certain characteristics to best serve you through your situation.

Animal guides are a strong essential part of Shamanism. Shamanism is an ancient spiritual practice that involves a person reaching altered states of consciousness to connect to the spirit world. This altered state of consciousness is usually attained by journeying. Journeying is a deep state of meditation that allows the individual to connect to the spirit world for communication. Drumming circles are usually incorporated into a journey as it brings in the rhythm of Mother Earth. Shamans are deeply connected to the earth and the spiritual connections within nature. Animal guides are followed and cherished amongst Shamans as these animals hold great truths and strength to help us through our journey.

If you are truly interested in meeting one of your animal guides, I strongly suggest finding a psychic center or Shaman in your area that can lead you through journeying. It's really a joyful, exciting, and honorable experience to meet your animal guides. Meeting your power animals or message animals isn't always easy. It may take a few sessions to clear your mind, calm your emotions, and trust your intuition enough to meet your animal guides, but it's certainly something everyone has the power to accomplish.

Like meeting your animal guides, you have the ability to meet your main guides and lesson guides as well. The best way to meet your guides at first is through a guided mediation. Just like in a journey, the guided meditation will take you into an altered state of consciousness that allows you to open up spiritually to your guides. You can find several types of guided meditations through psychic centers, books, spiritual magazines, videos, or through online resources. Connecting to our spiritual guides and teachers has become easier and more available than ever before.

By connecting to your guides on the other side, you gain insights and a deeper understanding of your connection to spirit, the Divine, and to each other. We are all here in the physical world, together sharing our unique journey with those around us. We're all connected through our conscious thought and our connection to the Divine. Isn't it interesting how many people all around the world can have the same realization or understanding about something around the same time without ever meeting or discussing it? It's because we are all connected spiritually. We are not physical beings experiencing a spiritual journey; we are spiritual beings experiencing a physical journey. How we connect to each other, the Divine, and to our spiritual self is best described through the Gold and Silver Cord theories.

## Gold Cord

The Gold Cord is our individual connection to the Divine. The Divine energy is a higher energy source connected to everyone and everything. This Gold Cord comes down from the Divine, connects to you, and radiates from within you. Some call it the white light from within or your Divine spark. It's our connection to a higher consciousness and understanding. Because this Gold Cord connects you to the Divine energy, which is connected to everyone else, you are then connected to everyone as well. This Gold Cord can never be broken, as it is your eternal connection to the Divine.

## Silver Cord

Our Silver Cord is our connection to our physical body. It's our soul's connection to our physical form that allows us to connect to the physical world. Our Silver Cord can weaken through medical illness or emotional trauma. This cord is broken once the soul leaves the body through death.

Our Silver Cord can be weakened by transient states or "in between" states. In life, we can be caught in situations that can sometimes cause us harm. This harm may be severe enough to injury our bodies into states of unconsciousness or to cause our soul to leave our body long enough for a near-death experience. States of unconsciousness are still hard to explain and understand. These states are usually found in someone suffering through a medical condition such as a coma. This is when our body is so severely hurt that it needs time to rest and heal. Our body seems to be in a sleep-like state, but your soul is still connected to your body. It's been documented that some people have experienced watching themselves in a coma-like state from above their body in the same room. This experience falls very closely to a near-death experience, but the person has not made any connection to their guides, angels, family members, or a white light. The pull to the higher spiritual plane has not been made; rather, they feel very connected to their lives and body. Their Silver Cord is weakened, but still very much attached.

Sometimes, someone can be in such a severe coma-like state or trauma that they experience a near-death experience. This is when the soul leaves the body and usually feels the pull to the higher spiritual plane. This type of pull can be in the form of a white light, a family's love, guides, angels, or just an understanding of a higher spiritual force and love that surrounds them. This disconnect from your body is made for a short period of time. It may feel much longer as time and space no longer exist for that soul. Near-death experiences may take you on a long journey to explore the experiences you had in your life. Most people come back from a near-death experience with a greater understanding of their life purpose. They usually want to change the mistakes that they've made and make stronger connections with people that they love. They come to a realization that life is much more than just the physical and strengthen their beliefs to become much more spiritual. Near-death experiences have been known to completely change a person after the encounter. Most have a more positive outlook on life and strive to live life to the fullest.

During a near-death experience, the Silver Cord of connection to your physical self is weak, but still connected. If

At the time of our death, our Silver Cord becomes detached and our soul begins to make the transition to the spiritual world. Because death and dying vary so much from person to person, the experience of this transition varies as well. Upon death, the soul is usually greeted by family, friends, loved ones, guides, and angels. These afterlife spirits help the soul transition to a higher plane of existence, also known as the "other side." Granted, there are no sides to heaven and earth. One does not cross a distinct line into heaven. To say it's more complex is an understatement. "Crossing over" is just an easy analogy to explain the transition of the soul from the earth plane of existence and a return to the greater consciousness and energy level known as heaven.

Someone experiencing a very slow death over the course of a few days may have already made contact with their guides, angels, or family to prepare them for their transition. Their loved ones comfort them, stay by their side, and slowly help them find their way to the other side. This slow process may happen during times of a long medical illness, coma-like states, an injury that lasts for days and gets worse, and so on. Their soul makes its transition very slowly, allowing them ample time to prepare and feel at ease. The closer the person comes to death, the stronger the pull to the other side.

Those souls that are ready for death find themselves being pulled to the other side. Some people have experienced a white light or tunnel that guides them to heaven, whereas others find themselves surrounded by friends and family. Once the person makes the conscious decision to cross, she transitions very easily.

Although the transition is made easily for most, there are souls that do not cross over. These souls do not complete the full transition and remain earthbound. It's been thought in the past that earthbound spirits reside in the physical plane of existence. Where they remain is actually just above the physical plane, but still well below the astral plane of existence. The stage of transition determines which energy level the spirit resides in. Meaning, someone who just died will still be closely connected to the physical plane and will slowly pull to the higher and lighter levels of existence throughout the transition process. Those who make the full transition will move through these levels very quickly, whereas those who find themselves confused or scared during death will move very slowly. Because of this slower movement to the higher and lighter states of existence, the spirit's ego, mind, and emotions will get in the way and may stop the spirit from further movement. These spirits will find themselves between states of existence. Because the state they reside in is closer to the physical earth plane, these souls are known as "earthbound spirits."

## Why spirits remain earthbound

The reasons why the soul does not decide to cross are as individual as the person who has made the decision not to cross. Some common reasons follow.

### Fear

There are many different reasons why spirits feel fear at the time of their death. Fear of death itself can be overwhelming for the spirit, especially if they've been taught to believe that death is a negative experience. Religious, cultural, and personal expectations and beliefs can hinder the spirit from crossing over. In some cultures, death is believed to be negative, so sadness and fear are strongly associated with the experience. Also, certain cultures or societies do not believe in the afterlife, therefore, death becomes feared. Though the spirit's consciousness after death becomes aware of their soul's continuation once the person has died, the fear will sometimes remain and will keep the spirit from transition. Other than fear of death itself, the fear of judgment is a powerful reason for spirits to remain behind. The reassuring white light signals possible punishment for those who have committed violent acts and believe they will be judged upon their crossing.

## Anxiety

Those experiencing fear regarding death will most likely also experience anxiety as well. Anxiety can manipulate the energy around the spirit. Thoughts and feelings create energy manifestations around spirits. So, if a spirit is anxious due to fear of judgment, the environment around the spirit will become dark and negative, feeding into the spirit's fear. This negativity can overpower the spirit. Their focus will now be on their negative environment, and less toward the white light and their guides.

Anxiety isn't always created through fear; it can also be experienced from loss, grief, and through the protection of others. Anxious feelings for the safety and welfare of others left behind by the person's death can also be a deciding factor for some spirits. For example, if a parent or guardian of a child unexpectedly dies while caring for the child, the parent might likely want to stay behind to make sure the child is safe and protected. Some spirits do eventually cross over once they know the child is safe; others do not. Often they decide to stick around and stay close to their loved ones, even after the danger is gone. Anxiety can create a false belief that they are always needed and the spirit will remain earthbound until their fear and anxiety have subsided.

## Grief

Spirits grieving for their lost body may hold back from crossing over because they have a hard time disconnecting from their physical life. Changing from the physical to a non-physical form is usually a natural experience that most spirits accept right away. Just like any other experience, there are those select few that can't let go as easily and will stay very close to their physical body and their loved ones. It isn't until the earthbound spirit accepts celestial form that it is able to release its hold on physical life.

## Anger

Anger can be felt in many different ways by the earthbound spirit. Some spirits feel anger over the situation of their death. A rage felt that their lives were taken from them (victims) or anger at a loss of control over others (sociopaths, murderers) can be felt. Those spirits that weren't ready to die might feel anger at God for losing their lives too soon. They feel God has full control over the reason for their death and direct their anger at God for letting it happen. They turn their back to the white light out of spite and frustration.

## Emotional pain

Emotional wounds can linger long after a person has passed on. Unresolved emotional conflicts and issues we all struggle with are only amplified after we pass on, making it even harder to let go of the pain and move on. Earthbound spirits have a hard time letting go due to the overwhelming emotions that they are faced with. Counseling and emotional support are needed to help calm and comfort these spirits.

## Trauma

Traumatic death can cloud or disillusion the spirit from their guides. Some deaths can be so fast that they do not even realize they have died. Fast deaths include fatal accidents, medical conditions, murder, and suicide. These types of deaths can be very traumatic, causing the spirit to release from the body very quickly. This fast release from the body can leave the spirit dazed and confused. If you can, think about what it feels like to be hit on the head by a very hard object when your back was turned. Imagine how out of sorts, dizzy, confused, painful, and scary that situation is. The same is experienced for the spirit but on a deeper level.

## Guilt

People often hold onto guilt about a decision they made or actions that they regret taking against others. Some actions may have led to the pain and suffering of friends or loved ones. The experience of death usually prompts a life review or a "look back" regarding their life. This isn't a full life review that spirits complete on the other side, but rather a quick glimpse at the life they lived and the choices they made. Knowing that they caused harm to someone else may cause the spirit to feel guilt and shame. The slower the transition for the spirit to the other side, the longer the spirit has to think about these mistakes and negative choices. That guilt can be strong enough to cause the spirits to walk the earth, trying to reconcile their guilt or feelings of failure. It isn't until the spirit can face the decisions they've made and forgive themselves enough, that they decide to make their way to the other side.

## Holding onto earthly possessions

Greed and the insatiable hunger for material things can compel spirits to remain behind, unable to let go completely of the physical world. Addictive or obsessive behaviors are usually present before death and can continue in the spirit world. These behaviors are usually released once the spirit has crossed over and connects to a higher consciousness. Earthbound spirits have yet to make the full transition; therefore, their negative mentality of possessiveness and greed are still very much a part of their consciousness.

## Not ready to die

These spirits believe it really isn't their time to go and are in a state of disbelief that causes them to ignore the white light and beckoning loved ones, instead turning away in an attempt to deny what has occurred to them. Unresolved issues can influence the spirit to stay behind until they feel resolution over a problem or situation. Sometimes messages to their loved ones here in the physical world need to be made so that the spirit feels comfortable enough to move on.

Another reason spirits stay behind is because many people believe that when they die, they become someone or something else. They believe holding onto the life they lived prolongs their personality and personal joys. Many people get caught up in the comfort of the familiar. Crossing over doesn't sound appealing if change is involved. Once these

# 3
# Where Earthbound Spirits Reside

doors, or messing with lights will usually be displayed by the spirit. This may last for days, months, or years, depending on whether the spirit feels content to move on.

# The wandering spirit

Those earthbound spirits trapped in a dream-like state usually stay in or around the area of their death. Some of these spirits will continue on with their everyday lives, whereas others will seem dazed and confused, wandering around looking for ways to clarify their situation. These types of spirits make little contact with people. They may be seen in the form of an apparition or light orb, but try to keep their distance from physical energy that disturbs their perception or emotional state. Many hotels, restaurants, or other common areas will often have spirits wandering around. It's possible that the spirit either died in that area or they came back to the area to find comfort.

The question has been asked many times why some spirits seem confused and not aware of the physical people around them. The best way I can describe this is through the tunnel effect. We've all been zoned out or focused so strongly on something that we develop tunnel vision. This means that as we focus on what's most important to us, all other people, places, or objects around us become zoned out or eliminated through our perception. We tend to only see what is in front of us. The same type of scenario happens for the spirit. Their focus on their situation and emotional trauma is so strong that they can't see or perceive anything else around them.

Spirits in a dream-like state also have clouded vision and perception of physical people around them. These types of spirits are usually playing out some part of their life shortly before their death as if death never occurred. To the spirit, these events are perceived to have just happened, whereas here in the physical world, the events play over and over again for days, months, or years. We know these situations better as hauntings.

## Staying home

After death, many people will make the conscious decision not to cross just because they aren't ready to go. They know that they have died and have decided that it just wasn't their time to move on. They still feel very connected to their physical life and the people around them. Many of these spirits will usually reside in their own home, living out their daily life, or they might just stick around and watch people around them.

For example, one of my closest friends, who is also a medium, once lived in an upstairs apartment in a two-family home. She often felt the presence of spirit energy in the home. She came home one day to find a white mist hovering around in the corner of her kitchen. She walked in, put her things down, and sat down on the floor in the corner of the kitchen to attempt to make contact. She found out through communication with the spirit that it was of a man who had lived in the house years before. He and his wife were both still residing in the home because they just weren't ready to leave. They had fond memories of their life together in the home. They were a very nice old couple with many good stories to tell. There weren't any negative intentions from them, just curiosity for the new resident. My friend had recently remodeled the apartment and the spirits wanted to compliment her on her work. She felt comfortable enough with these spirits in her apartment that she decided they could stick around for as long as they needed. The couple was in no rush to move on for the spirit, which allows them to move around without being overly stressed or confused.

# 4
# Spirit Rescue: Communicate, Counsel, and Guide

t's well-known that not all spirits cross over due to several reasons, such as traumatic events or emotional blockages, that hold them back from completing their journey. But
how exactly do they eventually find their way? The truth
is earthbound spirits cross over only when they are ready.
Earthbound spirits have free will just like you and I. They
have to make the decision to cross over when the time is right
for them. This is either done on their own or by a rescue medium. Mediumship is communication between spirits of the
dead and human beings. Rescue mediums use a unique style
of mediumship that focuses on earthbound energy communication. Rescue mediums communicate, counsel, and guide
earthbound spirits to help aid in their transition to the other
side. This type of spirit work and communication is called
spirit rescue.

Spirit rescue incorporates many different styles, techniques, and practices. Some of these practices are communicating with spirits, clearing away residual energy, clearing
spirit attachments, and working with guides and angels. The
bulk of our work is through the communication, counseling,
and guidance of earthbound spirits. Rescue mediums work
with many different types of earthbound spirits. Some are
easy to work with whereas others require more patience. All
call for a personalized approach in their rescue.

## Just passing through

It isn't always necessary for a spirit to cross over right
after death. Some spirits wait a few days after death to make
the full transition. They are still feeling the pull to the other
side, but at very slow pace. This gives them time to connect
to loved ones and to look back on their lives. This is sometimes helpful for the spirit to release any unfinished business

or to say their goodbyes to their loved ones. Not every spirit is going to transition at the same pace, and rescue mediums usually are not needed at this time. These spirits do not need to be rescued; rather, they are just passing through. Those spirits with a conscious understanding of their situation will most likely cross over when the time is right for them.

## Just wants to stay

Some earthbound spirits have a conscious understanding of their death and choose to stay within the physical plane until they feel they are ready to cross over. The best example would be the couple in my friend's apartment. They knew that they had died, but made the decision on their own to stay in their home. They weren't ready to let go of their life together. Rescue mediums work very well with these types of earthbound spirits as they are more open and receptive. Spirits can get fixated on a situation and may wander for a while until they get a gentle nudge from us to help them on their way. Usually the medium is only needed as a reminder to the spirit that they need to continue on. If the earthbound spirit or spirits are not ready to move on, the rescue medium will accept their decision and come back from time to time to check back with the spirit.

## Emotional counseling

Some earthbound spirits weren't aware of their death. These spirits might feel overwhelmed with grief and pain. Coming into a realization of your own death can be just as traumatic as the death itself. Some spirits feel hurt and betrayed by God by allowing them to die when they had so much to do in their life. They weren't ready to die and have a hard time letting go. Some of these spirits may have had their life taken away at the hands of someone else. Murder victims can sometimes remain earthbound for a short time until they can face the fact that they have died. Many feel anger and grief around their death, and this can cause the spirit to become less receptive to the rescue medium. The medium may need to make several attempts to communicate with the spirit. This may involve several trips over the course of weeks or months. These earthbound spirits usually require more patience, understanding, and counseling. It's up to the rescue medium to understand emotional stages during this type of rescue. At first, the earthbound spirit can be in doubt. They don't believe that their life has ended and it may take time for them to come to terms with their death. This is certainly understandable, especially if they weren't ready to die. After time, when the spirit realizes that they have in fact died, they become angry and frustrated about their death. Anger can sometimes last for a while. It may take days for the medium to calm the spirit down and help them focus. Once the anger has subsided, the spirit usually becomes overwhelmed with sadness. Grief and loss are usually part of this stage as the spirit will have to let go of their attachment to their life.

Each spirit is different. Some spirits may try to bargain with God for one more chance. If they were to change their ways and become a better person, would God allow them to come back? Rescue mediums need to help the spirit understand that there is no going back and only through their transition will they find resolution. Spirits may feel anger again after this. They might not care about making their transition and will want to stay earthbound. It's up to the medium to convince them that their true happiness is found on the other side by connecting with their guides, angels, and loved ones. Again, this may take time and might be accomplished through several visits with the spirit. Once the spirit becomes more receptive to change, they will release their hold on their life and transition peacefully.

## Suicide

As hard as it is to think about, some spirits do leave our world by means of suicide. Usually, these spirits are rarely earthbound. The reason is because these people have chosen death over life. Whether from a mental illness, depression, stress of life, or traumatic emotional issues, they chose to end their life and transition to the spirit world. Guides and angels are usually aware and prepared for this situation, and are what I call "on stand-by." People that choose to leave this world on their own are often greeted by their guides and angels first to help comfort them and to shower them with love. Family and friends are then greeted once the person is comfortable with their new energy. It's very rare that people do not connect to their guides and angels during a suicide. Only when the person chooses not to connect with guides and angels do I find that he or she becomes earthbound. This can sometimes happen when the person starts to commit suicide and then changes their mind during the event. It may often be too late, and he or she will transition to spirit. Their focus will be on regret and grief. They may hold onto their life and loved ones so tightly that they cannot connect to their guides and angels. Rescue mediums will work hand in hand with the spirit's guides, angels, and loved ones to help them during this tragic time and to help aid in their transition.

## Messages

Rescue mediums work mostly through counseling, but also play the part of the messenger too. Sometimes spirits need to connect to their loved ones first before they are ready to cross over. Unresolved issues play a big part in these types of situations. Rescue mediums will usually receive messages to pass onto their loved ones from the spirit to help resolve these issues.

These cases happen frequently when the person dies unexpectedly. Usually these spirits will reside in areas that allow the spirit to get noticed by their friends and family. Messages from spirits will vary depending on the situation. Some spirits need to confirm that they are okay, some need to say goodbye, and others will need to say they are sorry for dying. Rescue mediums will work as the messenger by communicating with the spirit to obtain the information needed to be passed on. It's not always easy to find the recipient of the message, so investigative work may be needed to complete this service. It isn't like in the movies where the spirit will walk you up to the door of their loved one and ring the doorbell. You may need to do this work on your own. Once the message is received by the medium and trusted by the spirit to be passed on, the spirit will usually cross over freely.

## Dream-like state

Those spirits that are in a "dream-like state" often find it difficult to connect to the medium at first. They can get confused or aggravated by the presence of physical energy around them. Rescue mediums sometimes have to shift their energy to best parallel their energy with the spirits. This means that we need to join them in their dream. Rescue mediums will walk into the energy of the spirit and join in on what the spirit is focused on. Mediums can sometimes perceive a time shift or environment shift around them. They can communicate with the spirit on their level of understanding. The best way to be received by the spirit is by slow, gradual communication. Once the spirit feels more comfortable around our presence, we would then slowly pull their focus in and make them more consciously aware of their situation. This can be quite emotional for the spirit, especially if they weren't even aware that they had died. Again, the emotional steps of grief are examined at this time through counseling techniques. The rescue medium needs to come through to the spirit with patience and to comfort. Once the spirit feels comfortable enough to let go, they usually follow their loved ones to the other side.

## Help from family and friends

Sometimes the rescue medium needs help from the other side to calm and comfort the spirit. Rescue mediums can call in family and friends from the other side through prayer and affirmations. Visualization techniques are also used to help focus our attention to their energy. Mediums can step into the energy of the spirit and connect to all guides, angels, and loved ones associated with that spirit. All it takes is a thought of their presence and the family member will come through. The friends you bring in must only be used if the spirit feels positively connected to them. You may need to ask the spirit who they want to connect to. If they aren't receptive to the offer, you need to evaluate which family member would best be of service.

For example, the medium might have to counsel a little boy that became earthbound due to emotional trauma associated with sexual and physical abuse. You wouldn't want

be helped until they are ready to face themselves and their actions. This will sometimes take quite a long time. They are usually so engrossed with negative thoughts that they continue to harm and harass people here in the physical world. These spirits are the most common during a negative haunting. This means that the spirit will sometimes attach themselves to a person, such as in a poltergeist situation, or they will reside in an area they feel they can harm unsuspecting victims.

Though these spirits are negative in nature and harass people around them, they rarely cause physical harm. Spirits will harass you by causing fear and anxiety, such as by yelling or moaning, moving objects, messing with electrical systems, scaring you by standing over your bed at night, and so on. The spirit is trying to harass you through fear and emotional pain. Physical harm is forbidden as this crosses a line of spiritual law. I'm not saying that all the emotional harassment is any better, but it still allows the person a level of control over the situation. Physical harassment takes your control away, especially if you are so badly hurt you cannot defend yourself. These types of situations mostly happen with non-human negative entities. These entities are not human; therefore, they do not fall under spiritual law.

## Spirit police

Just like in the physical world, spirits are governed by laws and rules on the other side. There is a strict understanding that no spirit is allowed to interfere with the free will of others. This means that spirits cannot continue to harm you if it's against your free will. These laws are enforced by spiritual beings that are designated to oversee all spirit activity within the planes of existence. These spiritual beings are what I like to call "spirit police." Other rescue mediums may call them other terms, but I like to keep it fun and simple. These spiritual beings or spirit police maintain proper order and remove any spirits that are disrupting free will in the physical world.

It sounds easy enough, but truly it isn't. Your free will needs to be disturbed for the spirit police to get involved. Now, I know you're thinking, "Why on earth would I allow a spirit to harm me?" Well, it's because you just didn't know any better. If a spirit is harming you or harassing you in any way, most people believe that they don't have any control over this. They don't realize that there is any choice in the matter. Most believe spirits can do as they please, when they please, and there's nothing the victim can do about it. This isn't true at all. It all comes down to thought and intent. You have to understand and believe that the spirit isn't allowed to harm you due to spiritual law. Ask for assistance, and be firm when you ask the spirit to be removed. Your thoughts and emotions control the situation, not the spirit.

## How to ask for help

Everyone has the ability to ask for assistance when needed. Calling for help in the spiritual plane is very similar to reaching out for assistance here in the physical world. No, there's no spiritual emergency numbers to call, but there are protection prayers and affirmations that can be used to bring in spiritual assistance from angels and spiritual protectors. In order to use these resources, your free will needs to be taken into consideration. Though you may be experiencing harassment from the earthbound spirit, some people find this harassment to be exciting. Fear will sometimes bring a level of excitement and amusement for some people. Why do you think so many people are attracted to haunted houses and scary ghost movies? It's because most people enjoy the thrill of being scared. It isn't until the situation becomes out of control or too scary that the person wants it to stop. I'm not saying that everyone will enjoy being harassed by a spirit, but it has been known to happen.

Once you have made the decision to have the spirit removed from your space, you can ask for assistance from the spiritual plane. Positive affirmation and prayers are used along with a firm emotional belief that you cannot be harmed. (Prayers and affirmations are listed in Chapter 11: Psychic Protection.) You must control your own space and firmly ask the spirit to go. Just like you would ask a stranger to leave your home, you need to ask the spirit to leave as well. Please remember that yelling or fighting with the spirit will only make the situation worse. Feeding into the negativity will only make the spirit stronger, which makes the situation harder to control. Only the use of prayers and affirmation to your spiritual protectors are recommended. If you feel that the situation requires more attention from professional resources, rescue mediums, clearing specialists, and spirit release specialists are available. Rescue mediums can remove or clear away these spirits because we've been trained through psychic protection techniques and through spirit removal techniques that have been developed over many years. It's not recommended to confront these spirits without proper training or guidance from a rescue medium or someone specialized in clearing.

# 5
# Rescue Techniques

During my time as a rescue medium, I've come across several different forms of rescue work used by various other mediums. Most rescue mediums will have a specific rescue technique that works well pertaining to their individual gifts and communication styles. Certain rescue techniques require several participants to join together to initiate a rescue, whereas other techniques usually only need the assistance of one or two rescue mediums. For the most part, spirit rescue can be completed through two different rescue techniques: direct and indirect.

## Direct rescue

The first type of rescue technique which most people relate to through recent popular television shows is a direct rescue. This form of rescue works "directly" with the spirit in the area the spirit is residing. This is where the medium can work one on one with the spirit to help counsel and guide them as an individual. Spirits will usually search out rescue mediums for assistance or rescue mediums will be called into a location where a spirit entity is detected. The rescue mediums will then communicate, counsel, and guide the spirit to aid in their transition to the other side. For those spirits not ready to cross, the medium will then clear the spirit from the area by either an energy removal or by calling in help from the other side to remove the spirit. Sometimes direct rescue will incorporate several spirits at once through a direct group rescue. This usually occurs at a scene of a tragic accident or event that has taken the life of several people. Depending on the size of the group, several rescue mediums may get called in to be of assistance.

"Scene rescue" is another form of direct rescue. Scene rescue is a form of energy manipulation. Rescue mediums can adjust the perception of an environment or "scene" the earthbound spirit is experiencing to suit a more stable and positive environment. For example, a group of soldiers may be in a dream-like state in which they are in the middle of a battle ground. These soldiers may feel like the scene or situation is still taking place. The medium or mediums then need to manipulate the energy to change the scene or event to gain the attention of the spirit they are trying to rescue. This technique is performed by stepping into the energy and changing the vibration. The illusion of the dream-like state is controlled by an energy flow of conscious thought by the spirit. By raising the vibration of the scene, the spirit will be forced to change their perception to better mimic the new energy vibration. It's sort of like coming out of a dream slowly when someone is tickling your nose. You sense the tickle which starts to grab your attention, and you slowly pull away from the dream to become more consciously aware of the new situation. Rescue mediums will start to change the scene through energy stimulation. Taking them from a dark and dangerous situation to a more positive and brighter environment may help ease the tension of the spirit, making them more receptive to help. As stated before, for rescue work in a dream-like state, the scene manipulation needs to be handled slowly in order to gently pull the spirit back to a consciousness that can be receptive to their guides and angels.

Another form of direct rescue that I use often is through "viewing of the medium." Earthbound spirits that are consciously aware of their situation, but haven't been ready to cross can directly connect to a rescue medium and view the medium's perceptions, emotions, and thoughts to help the spirit through their own experiences. I will often have a group of earthbound spirits tag along and stay very close to my energy, viewing my life through my thoughts and actions. Spirits can adjust their perceptions through my conscious understanding. When I experience a situation that they can relate to, spirits are able to connect with my consciousness and experience the thought and emotion themselves. Experiencing these thoughts and emotions can help them see through a situation and help them release emotional blockages and trauma keeping them earthbound. Though rescue mediums are most likely to have spirits follow them around, anyone can have this type of experience. The earthbound spirit will follow and watch anyone they feel connected to. This type of rescue technique is not an attachment because the spirit hasn't merged with your energy; rather, they are only standing by to observe.

There are times when earthbound spirits will hang around rescue mediums for comfort and reassurance that they are safe. They may not be ready to cross over due to connections they have with their physical life, but still need comforting to know that they are not alone. These earthbound spirits will stay close to the medium until they make the decision to cross over.

## Indirect rescue

Some rescue mediums use indirect rescue techniques through circle groups. This is when several rescue mediums sit around in a circle to try to make contact with the spirit for rescue purposes. They can connect to the spirit by a system called remote viewing. Remote viewing is when the medium can see and experience the scene and situation the spirit is in from a distance. Mediums can touch in with the spirit's energy to gain insights as to why the spirit has not crossed over. When they connect in with the energy, they can make contact with the spirit. The connection between medium and spirit isn't as strong as direct rescue, but it still provides a valuable resource for rescue work. Many mediums aren't able to travel long distances to have direct communication with the earthbound spirit, so remote viewing is used. Having a large circle group increases the chance of communication with the earthbound spirit as this provides a stronger connection to the spirit. Having many mediums concentrate on the spirit at once amplifies the energy being sent to the spirit. Once communication is made, they can help the spirit overcome obstacles and aid in their transition to the other side. When the spirit feels ready to cross, the medium can call in their spirit guides, angels, or loved ones. Some mediums do not call in help from the other side; rather, they only tell the spirit to find the light and cross over. I find that this doesn't always work. Most spirits are lost because they cannot find the light to guide them through to the other side. Spirit helpers in the spiritual plane are always standing by to help the spirit. It's best to call them in for assistance so that the spirit doesn't get confused.

Circle groups can also send healing energy to the spirit and recite prayers and affirmations to help aid in the transition of the spirit. Spirits can pick up energy being sent to them so they can be somewhat receptive to healing and prayers. This may give them enough focus to concentrate and allows them to consciously be aware of their situation. Once they are conscious of the situation, they can then connect to their guides and angels standing by to assist them.

A common question I have been asked before is, "What is the white light and how do spirits find it?" The light has always been represented as a door or tunnel to the spiritual plane. The truth is the light is everywhere. There really is no door to the spiritual plane. The spiritual plane is all around us, just on a higher vibration. Once an individual dies and becomes just an energy source, their vibration changes to parallel the energy vibration of the plane of existence it wishes to reside in. Our thoughts and intentions guide the way. A bright light has been seen by many people who have had near-death experiences. The white light represents higher consciousness. Each level of vibration has different sounds and colors associated with it. The white light is the color vibration associated with the higher spiritual plane as white is the accumulation of all color. The white light calls to us because our soul is remembering its connection to this energy vibration and wishes to return to it.

So when rescue mediums bring in the white light to help spirits cross over, they are really focusing the spirit's attention to the higher spiritual plane. The white light appears once the spirit focuses on the spiritual plane. As stated before, the tunnel vision or dream-like state the spirit is experiencing hides this white light from the spirit's perception. It's always there, waiting to be recognized and followed.

## Prayer

Though spirit rescue is mostly conducted by rescue mediums, anyone has the ability to help earthbound spirits through prayer. Positive prayer is one of the most effective ways to help a spirit if you do not have training or experience in rescue work. Some prayers that are commonly used are:

*"Oh God, please send angels or spirit guides to help any earthbound spirits to cross over to the spirit planes."*

*"Dear Lord, please watch over those spirits that have lost their way and help them find the light that will guide them to salvation. Amen."*

*"Dear Lord, heal the broken hearted and bind up their wounds. Help them find the light and love the soul so deserves. Watch over them and guide them to salvation."*

If you do not feel comfortable with a rescue prayer, feel free to create your own as long as they are coming from a place of love and support.

# 6
# Residual Energy

Most of us have had some kind of unexplained paranormal experience or at least we think we have. What this means is that we have experienced an unusual feeling or sensation that makes us believe that we are being visited or watched by someone or something that is in spirit. Most people believe that these feelings are from their loved ones in heaven coming in to say hello. Though it's true that we are being watched by loved ones in spirit who come back from time to time to observe, it isn't often that these vibrations are noticed and acknowledged. People mainly do not pick up on the signs and signals of these spirits because the vibration of their energy is usually pretty light and can get overlooked easily. For the average person, the type of energy that gets noticed is a lower, stronger, and denser vibration. It's the heavy feeling you get when you think you are being watched or when you feel there is someone in the room with you, though you cannot see them. This type of feeling would be the most common reason why people believe that their house is haunted. It's easy to jump to conclusions and believe that there is a spirit presence around, but there are other reasons and circumstances to justify these heavy vibrations. The most common reason I want to discuss is the vibration of residual energy.

Residual energy can be explained in many different ways and has many different terms associated with it. "Residual thread" or "time placement" are two common terms used by other mediums or psychics in the field. I like to use the term "residual energy," as I believe that this term best describes what is taking place and why the energy is still present. Residual energy, unlike an intelligent haunting, does not result from the presence of spirit activity; rather, it is the result of an emotionally charged event that leaves its "residual" mark or imprint on a space. This residual mark or vibration is left behind after a moment of high tension or emotional trauma. Residual energy can also be explained as stored energy from an event that gets released through time resulting in a display of the recorded event. Also, the materials found at a location such as certain types of stone can greatly affect the amount of absorbed residual energy.

## Hand print

All of this sounds great for someone who understands time placement or residual thread energy, but the average person doesn't know how to interpret this information or compare it to the situation they are facing. The best way I can explain residual energy is by the "hand print" analogy. Imagine that you slam your hand down onto the top of a table. The force that is imparted to the table from your hand print creates enough residual energy to be left behind on the table once your hand is moved away. If you were to take an infrared/thermal camera and record the event, you would clearly see that your hand imprint energy remained on the table even after your hand was taken away. The force or trauma from the event left a residual energy on the table and will dissipate with time once the energy is no longer strong enough to maintain its shape or form. Depending on how hard you slam your hand down on the table affects how long the imprint energy is sustained for. This type of imprint can also be left behind after a traumatic, emotional, or stressful event. The nature of the event determines the length of time the residual energy will sustain itself before it dissipates.

## Argument energy

Another example I use to help explain residual energy is by the "argument energy" concept. Have you ever experienced a time when you walked into a room after someone was yelling or arguing and you can feel a tense, heavy feeling in the room shortly after? This is due to the residual energy left behind. The energy from people talking, yelling, and arguing over something in a room for a period of time creates a heavy, dense vibration due to the emotional trauma displayed by the people involved. This energy or vibration of the argument can be detected even after the event has taken place. The strength of the situation or nature of the event will determine how long this residual energy can be detected.

Going back to the hand print analogy—instead of the example being a hand print, imagine an event taking place such as a murder, suicide, or traumatic accident. This event can create an imprint just like the hand, but on a much larger scale. The imprint can sustain itself depending on the severity of the event until it dissipates with time on its own or is cleared by a trained specialist. This residual energy imprint is a non-interactive energy that can be detected by someone who comes into contact with it. It does not have an intelligence or consciousness like a human spirit; rather, it is only a residual image of the event that took place.

Residual energy can be described as "time placement" because it imprints the event during the time it took place, displaying the event over and over again each time you come into contact with the energy. Residual energy cannot interact with you, nor can it harm you. You may experience and sense the emotional trauma involved, which will make you very uneasy or scared, but the actual energy itself will not physically harm you. Residual energy can seem like a spirit because the imprint itself can be in the shape of an apparition or the energy can be so dense it may feel as if there is spirit energy in the room.

It's not always easy to understand whether you have residual energy or spirit energy around, so I've come up with three questions to ask yourself when faced with an energy or vibration you believe to be a ghost:

1. Does this energy attempt to make contact with you?

2. Has anything been physically moved around you when the energy is around?

3. Does the energy make you feel threatened?

If you answer yes to any of those questions, then you probably do have spirit energy in your home or space. If you answer no, then you most likely have residual energy.

## Clearing residual energy

Many areas have some sort of residual energy. Again, the severity of the event determines the amount of residual energy left behind. Just like any other energy vibration, residual energy can be changed. You can add to it, remove energy, reform, or clear this energy from your space. Typically, people are looking to clear the energy so they no longer sense the vibration of the event that created the imprint. Most residual energy can be intimidating and scary. Residual energy is usually formed through negative emotions or trauma and you will pick up on those emotions every time you come into contact with it. It's best to clear away this energy to allow for a more positive and peaceful energy flow.

There are many ways to clear away residual energy. I like to call this "cleaning house." This means to clear away and clean out all the residual energy left behind through various clearing techniques used by many different mediums, psychics, and clearing specialists.

## Step one—Smudging

One of the best ways to start clearing out residual energy is through smudging. As described in Chapter 11, smudging is a form of energy cleansing by burning herbs or incense to create smoke in the air that stabilizes and equalizes the energy in your space. It's best to smudge every room in your space as energy can and will move throughout the building as you smudge. If you are working outside and it's possible to find a safe area, build a fire and let the smoke fill the air around the space you are trying to clear. (Remember to look into burning permits in your town.)

## Step two—Tools

The next step to start clearing the area is through crystal grids or just by placing crystals throughout the space to help raise the vibration of the area. If working outside, just wear the crystals if possible or place them in a circle around the area you are trying to clear.

Salt is also a great way to help neutralize negative energy. Salt is a mineral which is known for its capability to extract, which is why it's a great tool for clearing unwanted energy and in raising the vibrational levels in your space. Try to place salt crystals, salt lamps, or anything made from salt in doorways or windows.

## Step three—Visualization

Next comes the tricky part, because it's going to take some visualization. Often, people can sense the vibration of residual energy and can sense where the energy is coming from. Other people simply can't. Depending on your experience level, try to imagine the energy as a big ball of energy (like a big ball of gas, for example). Take your hands and visual yourself pushing this ball of energy out of the building. If you do not have windows around you, imagine pushing the energy out through the walls or down through the floor into the ground.

Another great visualization tool that works well, especially working outdoors, is to visualize the energy becoming smaller and smaller. With your hands, push in the energy and form it into a small ball. Take your hands and place them around the small ball of energy and visualize this energy dissipating in your hands by getting smaller and smaller until it becomes only a speck of dust. Allow this speck of dust to float away freely or imagine it disappearing away into something so small it cannot be seen. Either way works well, depending on what you are comfortable with.

I find it's best to clean your space physically after you have cleared. Cleaning and sanitizing your space after a clearing will help eliminate any remaining residual energy. Soap and water are great, as this removes residue and dirt that may trap and hold residual energy. Cleaning your space also raises the vibration in your space because psychologically, you feel refreshed and renewed.

Always remember to be grateful and thank your guides, angels, and protectors as they are working with you to help clear away your space. Be sure to say a prayer or affirmation that states that your energy is now cleansed and will continue to be cleansed as you see fit.

Depending on the severity of your residual energy, you may need to cleanse for a few days. I always recommend three days as this represents a cycle: one day to open, second day to affirm, third day to close. If you still feel that you have not cleared away all the energy after you complete these steps, be sure to contact a clearing specialist who is properly trained and who can help you remove all residual energy.

## Clearing yourself

Most of the time when you are working with residual energy, you concentrate on clearing energy from your space. Often we forget to clear ourselves. You absorb residual energy just as much as the objects in your space, so it's important to remember to clear yourself after every spirit clearing. Just like the techniques you used in space clearing, you would use these techniques for yourself and others around you.

Smudging yourself with sage or incense is a good way to help neutralize your energy. You can either sit in the middle of the smoke from the burning sage or you can have someone fan it over you. I always recommend smudging as a clearing technique, especially after ghost hunting or spirit investigation. Walking through cemeteries, hospitals, or historical landmarks can leave residual energy on your body as well. Smudging is a great, quick way to cleanse yourself after being exposed to negative energy.

Visualization techniques can also be a great way to help cleanse your aura from residual energy. Take time to sit comfortably and meditate for a few minutes. Take a few deep breaths to calm yourself enough to get into a peaceful

mindset. Allow yourself to relax and slowly go into a visualization for healing. One of the best visualizations I use to
help cleanse my energy is the "waterfall."

*Sense, feel, or imagine yourself in a forest surrounded by
trees and grass. In front of you is a large shimmering lake with
clear, cleansing water. Over to the left of this lake are rocks,
a cliff, and a small waterfall, showering water into the lake.
Step into the lake slowly and feel yourself in the cold, clear
water. Feel the water all around you, cleaning off all your wor-
ries, fears, and anxiety. Swim over to the waterfall and slowly walk up the rocks so that you are standing just under the
water. Allow the water to flow over you like a shower. Imagine
the water cleansing you from the inside out, penetrating deep
within your soul. You will now begin incorporating your aura
colors to help cleanse your chakras. Imagine the running water
showering down upon you becoming a deep red color. Allow
this red water to flow all around you from the tip of your head
all the way down to your toes. Absorb this red color within
you.*

*Once you feel ready, start to imagine this red color becom-
ing a bright orange color. Allow this orange color to flow all
around you as well. Let the orange color penetrate through
you. The water will slowly start to change into a bright yellow
color. Allow this to flow all around you and within you. Start
to feel your energy vibration rising from within. You feel more
positive and peaceful. Imagine this water slowly changing into
a deep green color. This color is especially important for healing. Allow this color to flow around you and through you until
you feel the full effect of its healing energy. Imagine this deep
green color slowly becoming a bright, vivid blue color. Imagine
this sky blue color cleansing over you and all around you. Let
this beautiful blue color penetrate through you. This sky blue*

*color will start to change and become a deep indigo color. This color is a wonderful color to help stimulate your psychic energy. This color is important, as this will help cleanse your intuitive mind. Allow this deep indigo color to become a bright violet color. This color is used to help cleanse your spiritual connections. Because you may have been working with spiritual energy, this color is especially important. Allow it to flow over you and through you. Now that we have cleared all the residual energy from your aura, you will end your cleansing with the color white. White is a clean, spiritual, and cleansing color to help remove all remaining residual energy. I always like to finish with the color white as it symbolizes Divine energy for extra protection.*

*Slowly and carefully, walk out of the showering waterfall back into the lake. Allow yourself time to swim freely and enjoy the peaceful setting of the forest. When you are ready, slowly walk out of the lake and lie down on the grass, allowing the sun to shine down upon you. Allow the sunlight to shine over you and through you, warming and drying off your body. You are now clean and clear of any residual energy. Take as much time as you need to lay in the sunlight. Fall asleep, watch the sky, or listen to the sounds of the forest—whatever you feel is best. You can end your visualization when you are comfortable.*

You can also do this visualization while taking a shower. I recommended using an Epsom salt and soap mixture when taking your shower. Wash this mixture all over your body as salt is a great cleanser for residual energy. Complete the visualization in the shower. When you imagine each color washing through you, imagine it pushing out the residual energy through your feet into the drain.

Always remember to cleanse your animals in your space as well, as they will absorb residual energy too. Smudging them slightly with a hands-on healing approach is best. Lay your hands on your animal or hold your animal in your arms. Use the same visualization, but imagine your animal with you. Or, you can imagine your hand pushing the residual energy from within your animal, out through its paws, feet, or hands. If you have fish, it's best to clean out the bowl and slowly add clean water. Remember to only change about 1/4 of the water at a time so that the fish isn't shocked by the new water.

# 7
# Spirit Attachments

There has been much speculation about what exactly a spirit attachment is. Many people believe attachments are negative entities whereas others believe they are evil earthbound spirits looking to emotionally or physically harm you. Although both statements are true, they aren't the only reasons why spirits would attach themselves to you, nor are they the only type of spirits that attach.

Those earthbound spirits that have decided not to cross over for conscious reasons, meaning, they made the choice on their own, can sometimes stay very close to an individual, or even attach to the person's energy for comfort. They will search out and find individuals that remind them of someone they knew or who they find an energy attraction to. Like energy attracts like energy. If you like baseball and play a lot of sports, you may find the spirit of a young boy who loved baseball attached to you because he finds comfort in someone similar to him. He wouldn't be attached to you for negative or harassing reasons; rather, he attaches out of fear and loneliness. The attachment of the young boy will eventually release once he feels emotionally strong enough to cross over.

Other types of attachments from earthbound spirits are those who seem very confused and lost. They will attach to people out of fear. These spirits may not understand that they have died and are looking for some sort of resolution and clarity for their situation. Again, you might remind them of a person they once knew or attract them with your energy depending on your likes and desires. People have asked why any of these spirits would actually attach to a person and not just wander around with someone. There are many reasons for this, but they usually attach because they feel the urge to connect to a physical life force to help them feel safe. It isn't until the spirit feels more comfortable with their new energy form that they will detach and wander on their own. These types of spirits could remain attached for longer periods of time because they need to make the mental and emotional connection to what happened to them and come to terms with the loss of their life. These spirits typically need the help of a clearing specialist or rescue medium to help them come to terms and aid in their transition. Sometimes rescue mediums or clearing specialists get help from the person whom the spirit remains attached to. The spirit has already made a connection to them and has bonded with that person. This bond can and will create a trust between the person and spirit. Once the spirit has made their full transition to the spirit world, the person is then cleared of any residual energy.

The type of spirit attachment that has been the most acknowledged and feared would be that of an earthbound spirit that is looking to attach to a person for negative reasons. These spirits are earthbound consciously and search out victims to harass and emotionally compromise out of anger, jealousy, fear, etc. I find that many earthbound attachments that harass other people were originally very unstable during life through various psychological issues. Their original problems of anxiety, depression, or obsessive behavior stay strong even after death and can sometimes amplify after death. They search out and attach to people that remind them of the person they were angry with or search for emotionally weak individuals to control. These spirits believe they can stay attached to their lives and life force by living through someone else. They can attach to that individual and experience all of their thoughts, emotions, and physical situations. These spirits can manipulate your thoughts and emotions to better serve their purpose of harassing you or someone else.

see this behavior as bad character for an individual which will imply that they are weak minded and easily controlled.

- **Taking pictures or videos in cemeteries.** The energy transfer from pictures and videos can attract earthbound spirits. Cameras produce an electromagnetic energy spirits feel drawn to. Spirits will either attach to the cameras which can drain the batteries, or they will attach to the individual. Spirits are capable of attaching to objects just as much as people, depending on the energy source.

- **Playing with spiritual tools like tipping tables or Ouija boards.** These tools are used for spirit communication, which more commonly attracts lower level spirits. Without proper psychic protection techniques, the individual becomes vulnerable to attachments.

- **Calling in unfamiliar spirits.** Trying to openly communicate with spirits without proper training or protection can leave you vulnerable to attachments.

- **Criminal acts/violence.** These acts lower your vibration whether you are the attacker or the victim. Violence leads to negativity, which in turn attracts negative spirits.

- **Ghost hunting.** Investigating ghosts without knowledge or protection leaves the individual susceptible to spiritual attack. Attachments are very common during ghost hunting.

- **Scary games like "Bloody Mary."** Games to invoke negative spirits will give you exactly what you are looking for. Negative spirits prey on the naïve. These games lower vibrational levels in your space due to the nature of the games. This allows negative spirits to come in and attach to an individual.

- **Continual exposure to negative movies or shows.** These movies are intended to entertain, but constant exposure can lead to dense vibrational levels in your space due to the nature of the movie. This can attract negative spirits.

- **Exposure to places of extreme human suffering, that is, mental asylums, hospitals, battlefields, and prisons.** Negative spirits will usually reside in places of interest with lower vibrations. Anywhere there's been exposure to human suffering, the negativity continues through residual energy. This type of environment houses negative spirits. Without protection, the individual is left vulnerable to attack.

## Clearing an attachment

These attached spirits need to be removed through various clearing techniques by a clearing specialist, spirit release specialist, or rescue medium. A clearing specialist or spirit release specialist is someone who is professionally trained to help clear away residual or spiritual energy from a person, place, or object. Clearing specialists will sometimes work to clear non-human negative entities from individuals experiencing a demonic possession or haunting.

During a clearing, the level of activity from the spirit will determine how long it will take to clear it away. The

individual's fear and anxiety will be the major factor in clearing, as the person must feel their free will is being compromised and must will the spirit away. That isn't always easy, as
the spirit will try to manipulate your thoughts and emotions
during this time. Spirit release specialists, clearing specialists, or rescue mediums must work cautiously with these individuals and help build up their defenses to become more
emotionally stable. Once the person can willfully detach
emotionally from the spirit, the clearing specialists or mediums can work with the spirit to help clear them or transition
them to the other side. Most spirits that attach to people have
emotional or psychological issues they need to work out with
the medium.

Some of these spirits are not receptive to help as they are
consumed by their negative emotions. These types of earthbound spirits need to be removed from the person and space
until they are ready for help. On most occasions, the "spirit
police" will get involved once the firm affirmation is made
that the individual's free will is being compromised. Angels,
guides, and protection animals will also get called in. These
spiritual helpers provide an extra form of protection for the
individual and medium. They will stand next to the medium
during a clearing to help protect them from becoming attached to the spirit as well. Angels and guides will also try to
communicate with the spirit to help them reform their ways.
Usually they provide an extra reassurance to the spirit that
their thoughts and actions will not be judged as a punishment. Rather the spirit will be accepted, counseled, guided,
and healed by their spiritual family on the other side. All
will play a part in removing the spirit from the individual,
counseling the spirit, removing the spirit from the space, or
aiding in their transition.

One of the most memorable experiences I had while I was training as a rescue medium was clearing an attachment of two spirits from a young lady. My friend and I were called in to help a woman that had been taking pictures at a cemetery for fun. She had spent the day there, taking pictures of headstones, trees, and statues trying to capture spirit activity on film. She had been alone, without any knowledge of protection against spirits. While taking pictures, she began to feel the presence of a man in spirit trying to scare her. After a while, she left the cemetery because the spirit's presence became too overwhelming for her and she felt very uncomfortable. Later that night, she started getting visual images of the bottom half of a little girl and the face of an angry looking man. She quickly concluded that she picked up an attachment at the cemetery and asked a friend for help. Her friend quickly called my team to come in to help clear the spirit attachment.

Upon arriving, my friend and I walked through the main door to the apartment complex and started walking down the hall toward the woman in need of help. The spirit attachment was very upset that we were there because it could sense that we were there to protect the woman from it. The spirit's energy could be felt all the way down the hall and tried attacking us before we even got half way. My friend and I quickly set up our defenses, adjusted our protective energy to reflect the negative vibrations, and continued our way to the door. The woman walked out of her door and the spirit quickly manifested itself to us overshadowing the woman's face and body. We could no longer see the woman, but instead, we saw the image of the man coming through her body. This was by far one of the strongest attachments that I had ever witnessed. The spirit hid from us once he knew that we were not intimidated by his presence. We all walked into the apartment to find the area very cold and dark with mist-like air all over her living room. Two bedrooms had open vortexes, and her cat was cowardly hiding under one of her beds. It was obvious to everyone that this spirit was serious about showing himself. Before the clearing took place, I quickly closed the vortexes in the rooms and started my protection rituals to help neutralize the energy.

My friend and I questioned the woman about her experiences. While she was talking, I could see the apparition of a little girl from the waist down standing next to her. The little girl was wearing a white dress with black dress shoes. The dress and shoes were dirty with mud and a dark shadow encircled her. I could tell that this child had been a victim in a terrible situation and died through the experience. The presence of an older, abusive man kept very close to the little girl. The older man was the spirit manifesting the negativity all around the room.

After a while of communicating with the spirit of the man, I discovered that he had sexually molested the little girl, murdered her, then killed himself, and kept both of them earthbound in the cemetery. The evil intentions this man had toward girls and women kept him at a lower vibrational level. Due to fear of this man, the little girl could not find her way to the other side. He kept her prisoner as he held her close to control her.

I was able to separate the little girl from the man long enough to disconnect his attachment from her. My friend and I brought in our spiritual team from the other side to help block him from the little girl. I was then able to bring the little girl's mother in from the other side to comfort her.

The little girl's mother was able to quickly protect her and cross her over.

While all of this was going on, my friend was completing healing work on the woman with the attachment. Healing work is through hands-on healing. The recipient sits in a chair and the healer stands behind them. The healer places their hands on the shoulders of the recipient to allow healing energy from the Divine to pass through the healer into the recipient. Hands-on healing can also incorporate protective energy to neutralize the energy within the individual with the attachment. This new energy stimulation caused the spirit attachment to break free from the recipient because the new energy being created wasn't at a comfortable level for him. Once the spirit was able to be separated from the individual, I called in the spirit police, animal protectors, and spirit guides to remove the spirit from the apartment. This type of spirit was not receptive to help. He was only looking to continue his harm and harassment of girls and women. After the spirit was clear from the apartment, my friend and I spent hours clearing away the residual energy. The woman with the attachment felt positive and safe after the experience. Before we left, we taught her protection techniques and told her to stay away from cemeteries.

Though the experience was seen as negative, it did have a positive outcome. The little girl trapped by the sexual predator was finally freed from her cruel earthbound prison. Without the attachment experience, she may not have been able to escape for some time. She now resides in a better place with her loving mother at her side.

## Something more than an attachment

Lastly, there are very rare occasions where a person will find themselves connected to a non-human negative entity or entities. This is not a spirit attachment; rather, this is more in line with a possession. Clearing specialists, spirit release specialists, demonologists, or members of the clergy are able to perform certain clearing techniques that best serve them. I personally do not perform these types of services. Demonologists are commonly used, as they work mainly with demonic energy. If I find an individual has this type of attachment, I immediately call in the proper resources. I have only experienced this once in my life and once was enough. I truly have respect for the individuals that perform these types of services. It takes a strong and loving character to provide this type of support. Anyone connected to or around an individual with this type of attachment must be cleared and cleansed by trained specialists. This clearing would be similar to a clearing of an attachment, but on a stronger level. Clearing demonic energy from a person can take time, through many sessions.

# 8
# Why We Feel Scared

Throughout the years, the public has been led to believe ghosts were generally evil in nature. The old ghost stories, movies, haunted houses, television shows, religions, and superstitions have socially conditioned us to believe that ghosts are negative or evil with bad intentions. This can make us fear the thought of coming across one. Just the words "ghost" or "spook" bring up a conditional response of fear. By allowing ourselves to play into the negative depictions of ghostly encounters, we are enabling the routine responses and common negative reactions. By opening up our awareness of the spiritual world and various forms of paranormal energy, we can become educated and re-evaluate our socially conditioned response with a neutral or even positive outlook.

If someone were to tell you that they think their house is haunted, your first response would probably be one of fear. But if the same person told you that their house is haunted with the energy of a young girl who is earthbound due to fear and anxiety from her detachment from her mother, you might be more inclined to be concerned for the spirit of the young girl rather than fear her. It's easier said than done, but I want to explain a few things about hauntings that might make you feel a little calmer or positive about the experience.

## Misconceptions

First and foremost, the amount of homes that claim to be haunted by spirit activity is so great that the chances of this actually being true are astronomically low. Millions of people have claimed to have had paranormal experiences in their home every time they think they've seen shadows, heard voices, seen lights, or felt uneasy. We need to calm down, re-evaluate our situation, and try to come up with other reasons why these things are going on in our home or space. Only in the circumstances that have no logical explanations would there be a chance that you have spirit activity in your home. I'm not saying that it's not possible; I'm saying it's not probable. There just isn't enough earthbound activity to go around. For the most part, people end up crossing over very easily and have no issues with death and dying. It's only in rare occurrences where people become earthbound.

As stated before, the majority of hauntings are due to residual energy that is left behind after a forceful or traumatic event. Many homes and spaces have this type of energy. Because people are becoming more aware of spirit activity and psychic phenomena, they are now picking up on this type of energy more often. Becoming educated and conscious of residual energy can help you learn how to neutralize or clear this energy. It will also help alleviate any uncertainty of spirit activity in your situation.

Due to the wider exposure on TV, people have also become more sensitive to spirits that have crossed over. A good many people can understand the signs and signals that our loved ones are coming in to check up on us or visiting us from the other side. By no means is this a haunting; rather, it's a loving visit from family and friends to check in on us. Spirit activity can be detected, but it's usually much lighter and focuses on positive communication. The only fear that you may feel is due to the social response we have learned to accept. Growing up, we were led to believe any spirit activity is bad. Religions mainly teach that ghosts are from the devil, which is evil and harmful. Spirits go to heaven, stay in heaven, and any ghost activity you may face is one with negative agendas. This just isn't true. The gap between the physical plane and astral plane is increasingly narrowing as our consciousness increases. We are going to experience more spirit activity as long as we are welcoming and accepting of their visits. If you aren't comfortable with the spirit activity in your home or space, ask the spirit to back off or go away. Your free will determines whether they can visit or not.

For those who do experience spirit activity that is consistent, overwhelmingly obvious, or feels heavier or denser, you probably have the energy of an earthbound spirit in your home. Again, this should not provoke a negative reaction unless the spirit has become threatening or negative in nature. Most earthbound spirits are looking for people and places out of comfort until they have resolved any issues keeping them earthbound. The aid of a clearing specialist or rescue medium can help in their transition or clear them from the space if they aren't ready to cross.

## Why heavy doesn't mean negative

There are times these spirits may seem negative, but it's only because they feel very dense or heavy to you. This heaviness from the spirit brings up conditional responses because we have been taught to believe that heavy energy is bad. This indeed can be true in some circumstances, but not in every case. To understand why a spirit will seem very heavy and negative is to understand "emotional baggage." Emotional baggage is a term to describe the emotions spirits carry around with them regarding issues they were facing at death or trying to face regarding their death. The more emotions a spirit is carrying around determines how heavy or dense the spirit feels to you. A lot of these emotions can be negative because they will generally focus on fear, rage, guilt, sadness, anxiety, loss, or hate. All of these emotions are heavy and quite hard to deal with. Anyone here in the physical world becomes heavier energy-wise when dealing with these emotions as well. So why wouldn't the spirit seem heavier while experiencing them too? They would, and in fact, they seem to experience it at a greater emotional capacity. These hard and heavy emotions are like bags that the spirit must carry around until they are relieved or resolved.

Though these emotions may be negative, it doesn't mean the spirit is negative. How often do we face emotions like fear, anger, or sadness? Does experiencing these emotions make us a bad person or negative? Probably not. We're still good people with good intentions. We're just experiencing a difficult situation. The same is true for spirits. It isn't easy for someone to understand if a spirit is bad or just has a lot of emotional baggage. It's really something that a rescue medium needs to evaluate. For most situations, spirits are good with good intentions, carrying around their emotional baggage. It isn't until the spirit becomes harmful or threatening that I would consider them to be negative or evil.

You do have, on rare occasions, bad spirits. And there are always a few bad apples in every bunch. They are few and far between, but they do appear from time to time. These spirits will search out familiar people, unsuspecting victims, or emotionally unstable people. The best way to deal with these spirits is to not become their victim. Release any fear you may have about spirit activity and know that your free will protects you against psychic/spirit attack. You have more control over the situation than you think and it's time to let these spirits know that fear will no longer be in control of you.

## Ways to overcome fear

Through the years, I've come up with a few techniques to help alleviate fear. First and foremost, the best way to overcome fear is to confront it. I don't mean to confront the spirit; I mean to stand up to your fear. Don't allow yourself to be afraid of something that you do not understand. Try to understand where your fear is coming from. Are you afraid of the spirit because they seem threatening, or are you afraid because you've been taught to be afraid? There are a few ways to calm your fear and feel safer in your environment:

- **Breathe.** Take in a deep breath and calm your emotions long enough so that you feel safe.

- **Focus.** Allow yourself to sense the vibration of the spirit. Do they seem scared, lost, confused, or do they feel threatening? Pay attention to how you feel; the spirit will communicate with you through your emotions.

- **Confirm.** Understand that this spirit cannot harm you because it's against your free will.

- **Think.** Should I be around this spirit? Should I ask it to leave? Do I feel comfortable with it around?

- **Believe.** Prayers and affirmations are great during this time as they provide you psychological security. Know that you have help on the other side to protect you and guide you through the situation. Ask for help or assistance from your guides, angels, or animal spirits if you should feel threatened.

- **Control.** Own your space. Only you decide whether the spirit can stay or not. Have control over your space and security. If the spirit seems threatening, tell it to leave.

- **Refresh.** Clear away residual energy through clearing techniques. Place protective items around your home if you feel the need for extra assistance.

If you feel threatened and you do not feel comfortable asking for spiritual help, call in specialists that deal with spirit activity. These specialists can clear unwanted negative spirits, leaving your home or space with a more neutral or positive energy.

# 9
# Forms of Spirit and Entity Activity

During a time of spirit activity, you might be faced with different forms of energy. Each form of energy serves a purpose for the spirit. Some spirits choose to be hidden, whereas others take a different approach. They choose to be out and in the open through visual shifts of energy.

One of the most common types of presence of spirit is through an apparition. An apparition is a visual appearance, often of a person or scene that is generally experienced in a waking or hypnotic state. Crisis apparitions, which are apparitions in which a person is seen within a few hours of a crisis or death, are most common as they have yet to make their full transition due to confusion or traumatic emotions. They are still very connected to their physical bodies and their focus on the physical keeps their energy heavy. Apparitions are ghosts, but not all ghosts are apparitions. This means ghost or spirit energy can be experienced through visual as well as auditory and physical sensory vibrations.

## Visual

Colors are common forms of spirit activity. You may see various colors such as white, yellow, green, blue, violet, etc. Spirits usually show colors as forms of expression. Each color has a different meaning. Color displays are very similar to aura color displays. Some colors do not apply as the spirit is no longer living, but most of them do.

Aura colors and their meanings include:

- **Red.** Active, strong willed, power or angry, thoughts of the physical body, adventurous.
- **Pink.** Loving, affectionate, romance, kindness.
- **Orange.** Creative or amused, ego, mental alertness, social status.

- **Yellow.** Inspiration, playful, intelligence, joy, freedom, contentment, playful, logical.

- **Green.** Healing or sending healing, love, peaceful, calm, restful state.

- **Blue.** Calm, comforting, communication, balance.

- **Violet.** Higher spiritual energy/guide, strength, success, raised vibration.

Other forms of spirit energy may be seen in the form of an orb. Orbs are usually seen as small, round, white or light colored lights floating in or around a place or event. Auras can be seen through orbs, so don't be surprised to see orange or red orbs floating by during spirit activity. Orbs are very common as they are one of the easiest forms of energy a spirit can take. Another visual form of energy may be through a mist, smoke-like energy, or fog. Fog or smoke-like energy is a physical manifestation of energy of the spirit. It's been known to be "the breath of the spirit." This is not to be confused with regular fog that comes out at early times in the day. Most ghost hunters or paranormal experts do research during late night hours that run into the morning. Fog is common during these times and shouldn't be confused with spirit activity. A mist-like energy will usually appear inside a building at various times of the day. It will appear out of the blue and dissipate just as quickly. This is just another way the spirit is trying to communicate.

Unfortunately, we do get visual manifestations with negative spirits or negative entities as well. These spirits usually take on a metamorphosis or shape-shifting appearance. The most common would be through a shadow-like appearance. These spirits come through as heavy and dark. These images are usually accompanied by negative feelings or emotions. Note, these emotions are not coming from you; rather, they are emotions and feelings you are picking up from the surrounding energy itself.

## Auditory

Other than the visual experiences we encounter with spirit activity, we also come across auditory experiences as well. A common form of auditory experience is through sounds such as "raps." Raps are a knocking or tapping noise heard by both you and the spirit. These raps can be used as a form of communication with the spirit. For example, when you ask the spirit a question, one rap equals yes, whereas two raps equals no. Raps can also be used for counting and going through the alphabet to communicate with words. Some people have experienced a bell-like sound that can also be used as a form of communication.

Buzzing or static noises can be detected, especially when there is a lot of electromagnetic energy around. Various electronic equipment can give off radio waves or electronic vibrations. Spirit energy can work well with these energy vibrations and play off of them to communicate. Spirits can join or merge with the electronic energy to stimulate its pulse, frequency, or vibration as a form of communication. Electronic voice phenomena (EVP) is a great example of this type of communication.

Footsteps or voices are commonly heard during a haunting or paranormal investigation. The denser the vibration of the spirit, the clearer and louder the footsteps or whispers are. This type of spirit activity isn't meant to scare anyone; rather, it's intended to inform you that they are ready to communicate.

## Physical sensory vibrations

Lastly, spirit energy can be detected through sensory changes such as vibrations, dense or light feeling energy, nausea, hot or cold feelings, or vertigo. Spirit energy can be mostly detected through how you physically feel. Hot and cold spots are very common. Hot spots are usually created by animal energy or higher level spiritual energy. Spirit or earthbound spirit activity is usually felt as cold spots. This is because the spirit does not emit heat. The physical body is gone, which is where our heat is created from; therefore, our soul or spirit will be cold due to drawing energy from the area to communicate. When a spirit touches in with you or is around you, you will feel cool or cold. It isn't anything to be alarmed about. Spirits just forget that they are cold and will move in slowly to communicate with you. If you feel too cold, just ask them to back off.

Negative spirits can and will try to attach or psychically attack you and the best way to be alerted to this is through physical feelings. Sensing cold energy around you is normal, but when you start to get the feeling of a deep, freezing cold sensation that penetrates into you, the spirit is trying to attach. Feelings of nausea, dizziness, and headaches are known to accompany this type of situation. If you start to feel uneasy, sick, extreme cold sensations, or fatigue, leave the area and seek professional assistance immediately.

Another form of sensory experience such as vertigo (dizziness) or energy vibration changes occurs near a portal or vortex. Vortexes are areas of high energy concentration, originating from magnetic, spiritual, or sometimes unknown sources. Portals are spiritual doors through which spirits or entities can travel in and out. These doors feel very heavy and are mostly associated with non-human negative entities. Human spirits do not need doors, but can use these portals when they are available. Portals are usually created through manifestations of negative affirmations. Conjuring up negative energy will create vortexes or portals.

## Misinterpretations

Many people have misinterpreted paranormal activity when they experience a sensory disturbance. Nausea, dizziness, headaches, and mental confusion have been known to be associated with paranormal activity, especially when the spirit merges with your energy or when you walk through the energy of a spirit. These symptoms can also be associated with natural occurring fields of energy and electrical sources. It's best to look for the most logical reason for these sensory disturbances before you jump to conclusions.

Dizziness, nausea, mental confusion, loss of coordination, headaches, depression, anxiety, and paranoia can also be sensed around high electromagnetic energy such as electrical wires, cables, satellite towers, or power grids. It's best to check with an EMF detector if available to confirm this. If you do not have an EMF detector, you can call in the electrical company to check for you. It's best to measure these electromagnetic waves. High levels of electromagnetic energy can cause temporary illness and long-term health problems.

Ley lines can also cause dizziness, nausea, and headaches. Ley lines are natural fields of magnetic energy underneath the ground. Birds and animals use ley lines as navigational guides during migration. People who are very sensitive to energy can often detect these lines as well. It's been thought that psychic energy can be amplified around ley line energy sources especially at intersecting points. Many metaphysical professionals believe portals or vortexes are in or around ley line activity. Nothing has been scientifically proven; therefore, believe what feels right for you.

Lastly, fault lines around the world have been known to create symptoms similar to encountering negative energy due to large amounts of energy generated from the friction of tectonic plates.

# 10
# Spirit Communication Tools

Spirit communication has been widely accepted by many different religions and cultures. The Spiritualist religion was originally founded through the belief of communication with the spirit world. Spiritualists would originally communicate through sounds such as raps or knocking noises. These raps would slowly evolve into an alphabetic dialog between the medium and the spirit. Through raps, the spirit was able to speak and give messages to their loved ones. Through time, more and more people became enchanted and mesmerized by spirit communication leading to the evolution of sophisticated tools used to supplement the raps or knockings.

Table tipping is a popular form of communication with spirits through various religious groups. Table tipping is a way to communicate with spirits through the use of a small, round, three-legged table. Several participants would sit around the table with their fingers lightly touching the ends of the table. The participants would then ask the spirit yes or no questions. The spirit would tip the table once for yes and twice for no. The alphabetic system of communication would also be used as the table can tip while the participants say the letters of the alphabet. The table would then stop on the letter the spirit wanted to express. From this, spirits and participants could form words and sentences to communicate more effectively.

Ouija boards have become one of the most popular sources of spirit communication in the world, with even a movie named after it. The Ouija board originated in 1890 as a parlor game and took on the form of spirit communicator when a Spiritualist added a divining tool several years later. This tool would be used by participants by holding the tip or end of the tool while it moved across the board. The tool would move over letters of the alphabet, spelling out words to communicate with the participant.

Pendulums have been used in the metaphysical field as a source of communication between spirits, guides, and angels. A pendulum is a weight, suspended from a pivot, which allows the object to swing freely. Most weights are made from crystals, wood, glass, or metal. Pendulums are held at the top of the string or chain with the weight suspended below. A pendulum grid can be used to help aid in the communication. A pendulum grid is a square piece of paper with a picture of a circle and arrows. The circle and arrows point to words such as yes, no, maybe, ask again, etc. When the pendulum is held, the weight of the object can move either back and forth, side to side, or in a circular motion. The spirit, guide, or angel will manipulate the pendulum to swing in the direction of the word it wants to express.

Pendulums have also been used over people, materials, or places to answer questions regarding the object in question. Many pregnant women have even used pendulums to try to determine the sex of their unborn child. The pendulum is held above the stomach, up and down movements represent a boy, and side to side movements represent a girl. Though pendulums are used primarily for spirit communication, they can be used for various sources requiring an answer.

Trumpets are used throughout Spiritualist churches, and mediums will use trumpets as a form of physical mediumship. Spirits can manipulate the sounds of a trumpet to physically communicate with us. It takes a very strong physical medium to manipulate the energy around the trumpet so that the spirit can manifest a sound. It has been known to happen on many occasions. When it does, it's a fun and exciting form of communication.

Dowsing rods are tools used to locate water, buried metals, crystals, rocks, and other natural sources under the ground. People have used dowsing rods for paranormal investigations as these rods also pick up on spiritual activity. Dowsing rods come in either Y-shaped or L-shaped forms. The person using the rods walks around the area in question with the dowsing rods pointing out in front of them. Once the rods sense natural sources or spirit activity, it twitches or moves to face the source. Someone using L-shaped rods will usually hold two of them, one in each hand with the longer part of the rod pointing out. When the rods come into contact with spirit activity, the rods will cross over each other. These rods are a very popular tool for ghost hunting. Though communication is harder to achieve with rods, the spirit can move them in several directions to indicate yes or no answers to questions being asked.

Although many tools are used, Ouija boards and table tipping seem to be the most popular amongst those who are interested in spirit communication. Though I support spirit communication, I do not support the use of tools without proper energy stimulation or protection techniques.

By understanding protection techniques, you need to understand vibration levels. Ouija boards and tables are physical objects. They have a lower and denser vibration than the spirit you are trying to communicate with. It is very difficult for the higher level spirits such as your loved ones on the other side to "come down" to the level and vibration of the physical object. Spirits with a heavier or denser vibration much closer to the physical vibration would be attracted to and have an easier time with communicating with these tools. These spirits would be the first spirits you would attract using physical objects. This would clearly explain the reason why so many people have experienced negative spirits or non-human negative entities during communication. These spirits will charm and entertain you. They will lie to you and persuade you into thinking they are someone else to gain your trust. Some negative spirits just flat out scare you and harass you from the start. These types of spirits would also most likely attach to your energy in the form of a spirit attachment.

## Protecting your tools

The best way to use communication tools is through proper psychic protection and energy stimulation. Energy stimulation is just like it sounds. You control and change the vibration of the energy around you and the physical object. The best way to start this is through prayers and affirmations for white light energy to surround you and the object. Visualization techniques are best used as they enhance your thoughts and intent to stimulate the energy. Imagine your vibration and the vibration of the object at a neutral level. This is neither negative nor positive. Put your hands around the physical object to stimulate a bond or connection to the physical object. Visualize your energy rising up toward the ceiling. Thoughts of love, joy, or humor can help raise your vibration. A feeling of gratefulness to spirit is also a great way to raise your vibration quickly. While visualizing your energy rising, recite prayers to your guides and angels for love, light, and protection. (Prayers and affirmations are listed in Chapter 11.) As your energy rises, the energy of the tool or physical object rises with you. Ask for only spirits with love and truth to come through to communicate and to ask your guides and angels to repel any unwanted, negative energy from your space.

High vibration crystals are a great tool to use to help raise the vibration of your space as well as the use of sage, salt, or other protection techniques you feel most comfortable with.

Common crystals used to help raise the vibration in a space are:

- **Aqua aura quartz.** Safeguards against metaphysical or psychological attack. It activates the throat chakra, which aids in positive communication. It is a healing stone.

- **Celestite.** Brings Divine energy into the environment. It promotes purity at heart and supports a calm and harmonious atmosphere.

- **Auralite 23.** Calms the mind and enhances spiritual awareness. It's great for re-balancing the energy in your environment.

- **Amethyst.** Encourages spiritual wisdom. It blocks stress and negative environmental energies. Amethyst raises the vibration of your space to very high levels.

- **Aurora quartz.** Master healer crystal, it activates all chakras up to the highest level. It raises the vibration in your environment to very high levels and releases emotional blockages.

- **Quartz.** Extremely powerful healing and energy purifier. It heals blockages and weakness in the physical body and aura.

- **Petalite.** Provides a safe environment for spiritual communication. It clears entities from the aura or the mental body, overcomes manipulation at any level, enhances the environment, and neutralizes black magic.

- **Selenite.** Induces clarity of the mind and accesses angelic consciousness. It's a dispenser and stabilizer for erratic emotions. It prevents against entities and negative energies and is a powerful healing crystal that resonates at a high frequency.

- **Herkimer diamond.** Powerful soul shield against negative energy. It's one of the strongest crystals for clearing electromagnetic pollution.

This type of energy stimulation takes time to learn and strengthen. Because of this, you may still get negative energy sneaking in to communicate and attach to you. It's best to use clearing techniques at the end of every conversation with spirits to maintain your safety and maximize your experience.

# 11
# Psychic Protection

Working with the spirit world can be a positive, loving, and healing experience. Connecting to friends and family as well as angels and guides on the other side can be wonderful. Valuable messages and information can be achieved through this connection as well as being able to heal emotionally from the physical loss of loved ones. It's no surprise that those in mourning have sought out more information about the spirit world and mediumship. Whether it's through books, movies, television, online resources, lectures, or classes, people are interested in learning how to develop their own connection to spirit. Individuals have decided to explore the spirit world through spirit tools, circle groups, mediumship classes, or on their own. Whichever course the individual decides to take, psychic protection techniques should always be a big part of the learning experience.

When thinking of the spirit world, we like to think of the positive side of things such as loved ones, guides, and angels with inspiring messages of love, joy, and comfort. Most of us come to the table blinded by love and with open arms, ready to receive all that is given to us. And for the most part, this is a great way to connect to spirit. But, on the other hand, this leaves us vulnerable and susceptible to psychic and spiritual attack if we are not being careful.

Thinking about the negative aspect of spiritual communication is never easy, nor is it a subject many like to think about. But, for those of us who have experienced the negative side of things, we couldn't imagine working with spirits without setting up our self-defenses and protection.

I've seen a variety of different psychics and mediums teach psychic protection techniques and usually they have a great deal of information that works very well. Most of the time, the teacher or medium tells you to imagine a white light of protection around you. They also explain that like energy attracts like energy. By concentrating on only the positive spiritual beings and saying your prayers and affirmations, the negative spirits will be kept away. I can say that this is a great start, but it's only a start. A great many of these mediums seem to forget that they've been trained by spiritual teachers here and on the other side for some time. They've learned how to raise their vibration, set up their defenses, speak their affirmations, and focus on energy they are trying to communicate with. They've had the time and experience to strengthen and mature their abilities. This is something that average people in the everyday world will probably never do.

## Categories for spirit activity

For the most part, I've found three main categories which people will fall into when communicating with spirits. The first group would be the majority, consisting of those who are interested in the spirit world for short-term curiosity, fun, and excitement. Ouija boards, tipping tables, séance groups, and paranormal games are their main sources of spirit communication. They aren't interested in long-term education or training with spirits; rather, they are looking for proof of life after death and possibly gain a sense of fear and excitement from the experience. Spirit communication becomes more of a game and less of a spiritual experience with loved ones on the other side. This type of communication is the most susceptible to psychic attack.

The second category would be those who are interested in spirit communication and look to educate themselves further through books, lectures, or mediumship gallery readings. These people have expressed an interest in spirit communication, but aren't looking to develop their abilities to assist others in communicating with spirits; rather, they are looking to explore and strengthen their union with their loved ones, guides, and angels.

The third category would consist of those who are interested in studying and developing their own abilities of mediumship and educate themselves further through books, classes, spirit-circle groups, and development circles. By developing their own unique style of psychic skills and mediumship, they can achieve a greater understanding of the spirit world and use this knowledge to be of assistance to others in need. Those in the third category often become healers, mediums, spiritual teachers, and spiritual counselors.

Whether you choose to expand your understanding of the spirit world through mediumship development or by experiencing the spirit world through games and exciting activities, psychic self-defense and protection should always be utilized when working with spirits.

Psychic protection is energy stimulation through tools, prayers, and confirmations that help raise the vibration of the energy within you and the area to help protect against unwanted negative energy. Psychic protection can be learned through various techniques and practices. The best type of protection would be the type that serves the individual the best. Not everyone is going to be comfortable saying prayers, creating protection crystal grids, or meditating to their angels for protection. Everyone will have their own comfort level; therefore, each individual should expand their knowledge of protection techniques, utilize the one that works best for them, and develop it enough to be used effectively.

# Protection techniques

Everyone has their own unique style, focus, and comfort level when working with spirits. Different mediums and teachers have different ways to teach protection. As for myself, I like to keep it simple and effective. Because psychic protection techniques can be quite extensive and lengthy in detail, I've listed a handful of resources to use along with general information to help you understand several forms of protection that might serve you best.

Those of you who are ready to communicate for short periods of time for excitement and adventure should be concentrating on protection techniques that work quickly, such as smudging, prayers, crystals, and candles. For those individuals that will be working with spirits on a continual basis, you should utilize tools and techniques that maintain a continuous flow of neutral or positive energy such as protection grids, salt crystals, mirrors, protection crystals, prayers, and affirmations. You should also be working closely with your guides, angels, and animal spirits. All protection techniques can be used by anyone at any time, depending on your comfort level.

## Protection grids

Protection grids are a great way to protect the energy of your home or business. Protection grids can be set up for days, weeks, or months without having to be recharged, smudged, or cleared. Protection grids are grids that have crystals aligned in a geometric pattern to cleanse, clear, and protect from negative energy. Different types of crystals can be used, as shown in the previous chapter. Selenite, quartz, black onyx, and agate crystal are the most popular. Leave these grids out in open spaces to allow the energy to flow freely and to clear away dense, negative energy. Since the grids can be set up beforehand, less time is needed to prepare for protection.

## Smudging

Smudging is a technique in which dried herbs are burned in a bowl, dish, or heat resistant object that can hold the herbs. Smudging wands can also be used which are herbs tied together like a wand. When the herbs are burned, they create a smoke that fills the air. This smoke should be spread throughout the dwelling by walking around the house fanning it into the air, into different areas of interest that need to have the energy stimulated. Smudging has been a useful tool to help equalize the energy in your home or dwelling. If you do not like the smell of the burning herbs, incense can be used as long as it creates enough smoke in the air.

## Candles

Candles are a quick and useful tool in psychic protection as well. Candles should be placed at the corners of the room, as well as on a table centered in the room. Candles are a great tool to help with positive affirmations and prayers. It's best to start with a fresh candle and allow the candle to burn all the way through. This helps complete the cycle of energy stimulation. Many colors of candles can be used, as each color emphasizes a different meaning. For protection purposes, I recommend the following colors to help clear away negative energy by raising the vibration of your space:

- **Gold.** Prosperity, wealth, money, attraction.
  Gold is one of the highest vibrational colors that promote enlightenment and protection.

- **Pink.** Pink represents love in the highest form. Love is one of the strongest defenses against negative energy. It promotes a positive environment.

- **White.** This color is one of the strongest colors for protection. It helps purify and heal. This color represents truth, protection, peace, purification, and spirituality.

- **Ivory.** This color is a soothing neutral energy and provides balance within your aura and environment.

- **Silver.** This color is used primarily for the removal of negativity. It is also a color associated with victory and stability.

- **Violet.** This color presents strength, success, and higher spiritual energy. This color naturally raises the vibration in your space.

## Salt

As I've mentioned before, salt or salt crystals have been widely used to neutralize energy. It is a great form of protection to help stimulate elements in the air, creating a neutral vibration or energy in your space. Salt crystals left in windows or doorways work well. Other people have used salt to form circles around the area you are looking to cleanse and rid of negative energy. Do what works best for you and your situation.

## Crystals

Crystals are wonderful tools for psychic protection. Crystals have been known to be transmitters, receivers, and enhancers of energy. Each form and color of crystal can be used for certain types of energy stimulation. It's best to look for crystals that are specific to protection and clearing away of negative energy.

Some protection crystals are known to be absorbing crystals; this means they draw in and absorb negative energy in a space. I personally recommend placing them around your home, office, or area you need cleansed instead of wearing them on your body. For shielding and repelling negative energy from your aura and body, I recommend wearing high vibrational stones.

Among the best crystals to use for protection are:

- **Agate.** Agate is a great grounding stone that helps promote cleansing of energy. It has a very calm and peaceful energy that helps stabilize emotional imbalance.

- **Black tourmaline.** Black tourmaline guards against negative energy and clears blockages. It has been associated with the base chakra to help promote grounding.

- **Black kyanite.** Black kyanite is a protective and healing stone that promotes grounding. It has been known to be useful when clearing. It pushes negative energy down into the earth, clearing your body and aura.

- **Black obsidian.** Black obsidian draws off negativity and repels curses. It forces facing up to one's true self, taking you deep into the subconscious mind, magnifying negative energies so that they can be fully experienced and released.

- **Black onyx.** Black onyx promotes self-control, intuition, and protection. This is a strong absorbing crystal of negative energy.

- **Jet.** Jet promotes taking control of life, transmutes negative energy and alleviates unreasonable fears, guards against violence and illness, and grants protection during spiritual journeying.

- **Selenite.** Selenite is a high vibrational crystal used to help stabilize emotional stress and chaotic energy. It promotes a calm and peaceful setting in your home, guarding it from negative energy. It's used commonly in protection grids.

- **Smoky quartz.** Smoky quartz is a strong, protective, grounding crystal that removes negative energy by pushing it down and grounding into the earth.

## Mirrors

Mirrors have been used for years to help protect against evil spirits. It's been said that evil spirits cannot and will not look into their own reflection. Keep mirrors on doors, walkways, or places of interest in your home. Mirrors are also used to deflect negative energy back to the sender. It is a great way to shield your energy and aura from psychic attack.

## Singing bowls

Singing bowls, usually made from crystal, glass, or copper help stimulate the energy within you and your environment. To activate the bowl, a mallet or wand is tapped against the side of the bowl to start the bowl vibrating. You can immediately feel the vibration change in the environment with the first stroke. As it is vibrating, you then glide the mallet against the rim of the bowl in a circular motion to continue its sound vibration. Each bowl, depending on its size, will have its own unique sound frequency. Each frequency of sound stimulates different chakras. The higher the frequency of the sound, the higher the level of protection you have in your environment.

## Fragrances

Different fragrances can stimulate positive energy in your environment. All atoms in the universe contain a vibrational motion. Each motion has its own unique frequency. Essential oils are measured in magnetic energy. Different fragrances from these essential oils contain their own unique frequency. High vibrational oils help stimulate the energy in your space. Fragrances recommended to help stimulate higher vibrations are:

- Sandalwood.
- Jasmine.
- Myrrh.
- Amber.
- Frankincense.

As well as the vibrational changes with essential oils, smells from certain fragrances help calm emotional blockages and increase psychological joy. Angelic energy and higher spiritual energies are also attracted to certain fragrances as well.

## Music

Music is one of my favorite ways to help raise the vibration of your space. Not only do the frequency waves of the music change the vibrational levels in your space, but it also improves your emotional outlook. Music helps stimulate positive vibrations because it has a way of lifting your mood, make you energized, express joy, and heal your emotions. Music can make you feel good or bad, depending on the type of music you are playing, so it's best to listen to more upbeat and positive songs to help lift your mood. Inspirational and celebratory songs work best.

The frequencies in the musical notes also help stimulate the vibrational levels in your space. Those songs with higher octaves will change the vibration in the room; the higher the octave, the higher the vibration. Music is always a great way to raise your vibration and works almost instantly.

## Prayers and affirmations

I honestly believe prayers and affirmations are the best resources and tools for protection. Connecting to the higher spiritual sources for love, light, and protection is strongly needed, especially when working with spirit energy. Your guides and angels are here to help and protect you. They can't do anything without your request for the assistance as that would interfere with free will. Prayers are a way to ask for assistance. Always be thankful to your guides and angels for their help. Their love and guidance is a special gift that should not be taken for granted.

For those who aren't familiar with protection prayers, it's best to use prayers that work well for others until you come up with prayers you feel comfortable using. You can always create your own prayers once you've established a special relationship with your guides and angels.

A few prayers that are used often are:

*Prayer to St. Michael*

*Blessed Michael, Archangel,*

*defend us in the hour of conflict;*

*be our safeguard against the wickedness and snares of the devil.*

*May God restrain him, we humbly pray;*

*and do thou, O Prince of the heavenly host,*

*by the power of God, thrust, down to hell, Satan,*

*and with him the other wicked spirits*

*who wander through the world for the ruin of souls.*

*Circle of Light Prayer*

*The light of God surrounds us (me).*

*The love of God enfolds us (me).*

*The power of God protects us (me).*

*The presence of God watches over us (me).*

*Wherever we are (I am), God is.*

*And all is well.*

*Psalm 23*

*The Lord is my shepherd; I shall not want.*

*He maketh me to lie down in green pastures: he leadeth me beside the still waters.*

*He restoreth my soul: he leadeth me in the paths of righteousness for his name's sake.*

*Yea, though I walk through the valley of the shadow of death; I will fear no evil: for thou art with me; thy rod and thy staff they comfort me.*

*Thou preparest a table before me in the presence of mine enemies: thou anointest my head with oil; my cup runneth over.*

*Surely goodness and mercy shall follow me all the days of my life; and I will dwell in the house of the Lord forever.*

## Affirmations

Affirmations are declarations or statements affirming that something is true. This is especially important in psychic protection. Affirmations are a great way for you to declare your emotional strength and confidence in a situation. As they always say, "Say what you mean and mean what you say." The same goes for affirmations. Believe in what you are stating and trust that you have the strength and willpower to see it through.

Some sample affirmations are:

- "I am strong and brave."
- "I am protected by the loving light of God."
- "I am safe and protected."
- "I believe the power of God's love will protect and guide me."
- "I am surrounded by the white light of protection; nothing shall harm me."

## Protective animal spirits

Just like guides and angels, we can call upon our animal spirits to aid in our protection. We all have certain spirit animals that specialize in guarding and protection. Calling upon your protection animals takes training and development. It takes time to meet your spirit animals and build a relationship with them. You have them around you whether you are aware of it or not. If you haven't built a relationship with them through meditation or visualization techniques, I strongly suggest you call upon them to be of assistance, but not to work with them directly. For those who have met with their spirit animals, it's best to build a relationship with them so that you understand the gifts they are bringing you. Each animal offers a unique trait and quality. Learn what they mean and embrace this quality through your spirit work.

## Meditation/Visualizations

Meditation techniques can be learned through CDs, videos, books, lectures, or classes. Visualization is a mental image that you create with an affirmation and is a great way to connect to your spirit guides, angels, and spirit animals. To start your visualization, you can sense, feel, or imagine something being created around you. One type of visualization is of the white light of protection that many mediums like to teach:

*Sense, feel, or imagine a white circle of light surrounding your body. Everything within the circle of light is protected by the love and light of God. Imagine this circle radiating from within you and encompassing around you. You circle of light is your barrier to negative energy. Only goodness and love may come in and only goodness and love may go out.*

Keep this visualization of the white light circle around you whenever you work with spirits. Imagine this to be your door to the spirit world. Allow only those who can pass through loving light to communicate with you. It will take time to learn how to build and strengthen your white light of protection, but it is one of the best forms of visualization and affirmations to use.

## Raising your vibration

Learning how to raise your vibration is more for experienced students and those who are familiar with energy work. A vibration is a pulse within a layer of energy. When you think of vibrations and energy, imagine layers of a cake. Each layer has a different vibration depending on its density. With each layer of energy, comes a different color and vibration associated with this energy. Obviously a lower energy level will have a heavier, slower vibration and a higher energy level will have a lighter and faster energy vibration. Learning how to raise your physical vibration, which is denser and slower, to a spiritual vibration which is lighter and faster is achieved through visualization and meditation techniques. Once you have become stronger with these techniques, you can raise your vibration easily just by thought and intent. Some great tools to help raise your vibration are through singing bowls, bells, chimes, and music. Find the vibration you want to achieve in your tool and match your vibration to its level. Again, this takes time and training, but anyone can learn how to do this. The best way to describe the feeling of raising your vibration would be through the airplane analogy.

Imagine what it feels like when an airplane is beginning to take off. You start at a neutral point and slowly start to feel your body and energy pulling higher and higher as the airplane starts to take off. The change in cabin pressure as you ascend begins to feel lighter and lighter. When the airplane completes its ascension into the sky, a distinct change in the cabin occurs and the pressure feels much lighter; it almost feels like you are floating at first. The same type of feeling can be experienced through raising your vibration. A visualization I like to use to raise my vibration is "walking up the stairs":

*Sense, feel, or image yourself standing at the bottom of a large staircase. The stairs are pure white, escalating up toward the sky. Begin by stepping onto the stairs at the base and imagine all your fears, anxiety, depression, and negative thoughts starting to dissipate. When ready, start slowly walking up the stairs. With each few steps you take, the color of the stairs start to change. You first begin seeing the color red. The stairs beneath your feet are a deep and vivid red color. Allow this color to radiate up your feet into your body. You feel energized and strong. Keep moving up the stairs. Within a few stairs, the next color you see underneath your feet is a bright, glowing orange. Allow this color to radiate up your feet into your body. You feel proud and full of confidence. Take a few more steps up. The next color you see underneath your feet is a soft, crisp yellow color. Allow this color to radiate up through your feet into your body. You feel full of joy and feel energized. Keep moving up the stairs. You should start to feel a change in your energy levels; like the cabin pressure, it feels much lighter. Within a few steps the next color you see is a bright and lustrous green. Allow this color to radiate up through your feet into your body. You feel healing energy surround your body. All your anxiety, fears, and emotional issues are now gone. Keep moving. The next color you see is a beautiful sky blue. Allow this color to radiate up through your feet into your body. You feel calm and secure. Keep moving up the stairs. The next color you see is a deep and mesmerizing indigo. Allow this to radiate through your feet up into your body. You're almost at the top, keep moving! The next few stairs under your feet become a glowing, radiant violet. This color shines all around you, moves up through your feet, through your body, up to the crown of your head. You feel more open to spiritual love and guidance. You are now able to step off the stairs onto a platform at the top. At this platform you stand tall and strong, knowing you are fully protected and loved.*

Often, people feel more comfortable with the same concept, but use a ladder, escalator, elevator, or rope—anything that will help them visualize moving in an upward direction. Use whatever visualization that works best for you.

## Confidence/Control

I've mentioned before the different tools and techniques you can use to help protect yourself against unwanted energy, but the best form of protection is the faith you need to have in yourself. You need to believe that you have the power and free will to control the situation. Free will is a gift given to you that negative energy cannot take away. You need to learn how to gain confidence in yourself and in your ability to overcome obstacles that negative spirits will try to influence you with. Having control is key to maintaining protection not only around you, but around others that are connected to you.

Negative spirits will attempt to influence you through your thoughts and emotions. By having a clear and level mind over the situation, you can maintain a safe and protected energy level to work with spirits.

Always know that you are never alone. Spirit guides, angels, and spirit animals are always there by your side to help protect and comfort you. They may take a step back from time to time to allow you the chance to learn from your situation or to become stronger at defending yourself, but they will never leave you all on your own. By strengthening your faith in your own abilities, you gain confidence to not only help yourself through troubling situations, but also to help others in need.

# 12
# Non-Human Negative Entities

Though it's been thought in the past that spirit rescue incorporates demon energy by spirit releasement or demon possession as forms of our practice, in fact it does not. Spirit rescue is the communication and counseling of earthbound human spirits and aiding in their transition to the other side, not dealing with demon possessions or exorcisms.

Rescue mediums do work with human earthbound energies that have become attached to people here on the physical plane. This would be in the form of a spirit attachment. Rescue mediums perform clearing techniques or help the spirit cross over in those circumstances. These spirits may seem very negative in nature, and in truth, they can be. However, they are still human earthbound spirits and not non-human negative entities.

There are times that rescue mediums do come into contact with non-human negative entities or what other people like to call "demons" during a rescue. They are usually attached to an earthbound spirit during a rescue and can influence the spirit (which may be a big reason why the spirit has not crossed over). Rescue mediums that are comfortable dealing with these energies can call in assistance from the other side to help clear them or they can call in help in the physical plane from spirit release specialists or demonologists.

I personally do not deal with these types of energies. If I should find a spirit that has a non-human negative entity attachment or find the spirit I have come to help that is in fact non-human and not in need of assistance, I request help from release specialists or demonologists. Once the spirit has been cleansed of the demon, I can then work on counseling and rescue work with the spirit.

How can I tell if the spirit is just an earthbound or a non-human negative entity? The answer is in the vibration.

Everything in the universe carries its own unique vibration. Human earthbound spirits all carry a similar vibration depending on the emotional levels of the spirit. Human vibrations vary in degrees, but mainly stay fairly close in detail and in denseness. Vibrational levels of earthbound spirits change as their consciousness changes. As the spirit becomes more conscious of its surroundings and makes the decision to cross over, the energy becomes lighter and lighter until the vibration equals to the same vibrational levels of spirits on the other side. Those spirits that remain earthbound will continue to carry a heavy vibrational level depending on their emotional state. Earthbound spirits often have some pretty heavy baggage and can carry a very low vibrational level, but not nearly as low as demon energy. Demon energy is much lower than earthbound spirit energy and can be easily detected by a rescue medium.

Another way I can determine a non-human negative entity is because they feel hollow. The entity lacks the Divine essence that is within every human spirit. It's the light that radiates from within each and every one of us, regardless of the emotional baggage we carry around. It's our connection to the Divine and to each other. The non-human negative entity does not have this connection nor does it have the light from within. Demon energy vibrates at a very dense level.

Non-human negative entities can come in several different forms. They have a shape shifting ability which allows them to manipulate their energy into various forms. Some manifestations have been in the shapes of horned demon-like animals, large black spiders, human-like bodies with demon faces, etc. Though earthbound spirits can be seen in various ways such as orbs, mist-like smoke, or colors in the air, they generally do not change into these demon-like creatures.

Just what is a demon energy? Is it a fallen angel? Is it a manifestation of negative energy created by humans? Is it its own entity source just like angels, humans, or higher spiritual beings? No one has a definitive answer. It's been said that these energies were created by God, as they teach you love. How would you understand love and all things that are of love, until you experience the lack of it? It's true we all carry within us the connection to good and evil. It's our free will that determines our direction and the choices that we make. As harmful as the negative entities are, they are in some sort of way serving a purpose. Again, as enlightened as that sounds, I continue to keep my distance from these negative entities and encourage others to do the same.

Non-human negative entities are not the typical sort of energies you would find in your home or space. These types of energies have to be invited in by some sort of welcoming force. Like energy attracts like energy. These entities have to have some sort of attraction to you or your space and the vibrational levels needed to support them so that they feel invited. This doesn't mean that every time you watch a scary movie or talk about demons that you are inviting them in. But if you do have this type of energy in your home continually and talk about demon entities continually, then you are in part changing the vibration levels of your home making it more supportive of demon energy. Thought creates action. By thinking about someone or something over and over again, you can create it or bring in that energy from an outside source. This is the power of attraction. Just remember, when you focus on non-human negative entities for any length of time, it's best to change your focus and attract higher, lighter energies into your home once you are done by raising your vibration.

Here are some simple ways to help raise your vibration quickly:

- Smiling.
- Laughter.
- Thinking of loved ones.
- Being grateful.
- Doing something fun.
- Taking a walk.
- Taking a bubble bath.
- Singing.
- Dancing.
- Hugging.
- Eating something sweet.

If you feel that you have a non-human negative entity in your space, contact a spirit release specialist, clearing specialist, or demonologist in your area.

# 13
# Spirit Rescue Is Not Ghost Hunting

Ghost hunting has been around for many years and in many forms. It first originated as a way to debunk ghost inquiries and to contemplate other reasons and theories why people would experience paranormal situations. It slowly transformed into a widely accepted practice to educate and validate the existence of spirit phenomena and paranormal anomalies. Ghost hunters or ghost investigators walk around places of interest with technical equipment such as EVP recorders, infrared cameras, EMF detectors, spirit boxes, etc. with the intent to capture ghost activity. Though most groups have great intentions with the focus to educate people about the spirit world, some ghost hunting groups consist of non-professional individuals wandering around areas of ghost activity with little to no experience with the spirit world. Because of the lack of experience with earthbound spirits, ghost hunting is not the safest way to investigate spirit activity, as most hunters are not properly trained in psychic protection.

Typically, ghost hunting groups hear about spirit activity or get called into a place where spirit activity is suspected to investigate. Many ghost hunters will use technical equipment that was never intended to be used for the detection of spirit activity and claim to be experts regarding how the systems work and how they detect spirits. Though it's true that some of these tools do pick up on spirit activity, it's not the tools that work effectively; rather, it's the spirits that merge and collaborate with these tools that do the work. If a spirit wants to be detected, they will work with the electronic equipment to manipulate and stimulate the electronic waves to correlate a system of communication that people will understand. The fact that these tools work with spirits is due to the spirits' electronic or static stimulation, not the tool themselves.

I truly do not have any problem with professional teams working within a space trying to pick up on spirit activity in an attempt to educate and validate the existence of life after death. I believe it takes many different forms and levels of work to help people understand the spirit world, and I believe it's best that we all work together. There are a few personal issues I have with ghost hunting teams due to the experience I've had within the spirit world and the information I've received in training. The first and foremost issue I have with ghost hunting is initiating a response from the spirit by antagonizing it to the point that the spirit has to respond. Poking it with a stick isn't the best form of communication, especially with earthbound spirits. The emotional instability that these spirits have is the main reason why they are earthbound in the first place. Calling the spirit names or bringing up painful memories to provoke a response is not professional, nor is it productive to the aid of the spirit. I believe paranormal teams need to educate themselves more about earthbound energy and possibly work in conjunction with rescue mediums to produce a more positive and productive communication with the spirit. Ghosts were once people too and should be shown the respect they deserve.

Also, there are paranormal teams or ghost hunters that continue to exaggerate events and depict spirits as being negative and scary, playing upon the stereotype of the "evil ghost." We've grown up with ghost stories and paranormal movies conditioning us to believe that ghosts are evil, and this just isn't true. When it comes to hauntings, the event is usually far from demonic. Most hauntings are due to either residual energy, earthbound spirits that are lost and trying to find their way home, or a higher spiritual energy (a spirit that has crossed over) that just wants to be around you to observe. In the minority are earthbound spirits that have harmful, negative intentions, or non-human negative entities. For some reason, the smallest experience in a haunted location often becomes the branding of what it truly is, while ignoring the facts.

Continually filming shows or conducting investigations at night only plays into the social conditioning that ghosts are scary by making your environment or scene scary. I'm pretty sure spirits residing in that area could care less if the lights were on or off. Maintaining the spooky illusion of ghosts and hauntings is an unprofessional way to conduct investigations. Ghost hunting teams seem to be maintaining the illusion of fear to gain a wider audience so that they remain popular. Instead of the sensational, should focus on explaining the truth about spirit activity and trying to educate people about hauntings.

Though some paranormal teams work with rescue mediums to assist the spirit once the investigation is complete, most do not. They investigate, evaluate, and confirm whether there is spirit activity, but do nothing to assist the spirit or help clear the spirit from the area. This leaves the spirit or place without any resolution, leaving the inquirer just as confused as they were before.

Spirit rescue has been around much longer than ghost hunting and will continue to evolve as more people become educated and open to the spirit world. The main focus of spirit rescue is to come to the aid of the spirit. If spirit activity is not detected, clearing techniques are used to help neutralize the space. Rescue mediums do not need the assistance of investigative tools. Tools are used for more physical proof of the spirit rather than for actual communication.

If investigative teams and rescue mediums choose to work together, physical proof as well as resolution of the spirit should be completed effectively to better service the inquirers and the earthbound spirit.

# 14

# How to Become a Rescue Medium

Many great mediums have said that anyone can connect with spirits if he or she opens their heart and mind enough to the experience of spirit communication. I do believe that everyone has the ability to become a medium. However, I do not believe that everyone *should* become a rescue medium and connect to spirits through spirit rescue. This unique style of mediumship is for the select few, because working with earthbound energy can be very difficult. It takes years of training and development to become a rescue medium. I truly believe that I was born to become a rescue medium, and I've been training throughout my entire life in one way or another to build the necessary skills to excel in spirit rescue work. Working with spirits, helping them through their issues, and watching them continue on with their journey has been the most rewarding thing I've ever done. It's also been one of the most challenging as well. It takes a person with a level mind, strong heart, and brave spirit to succeed in spirit rescue.

If you truly believe the path of spirit rescuer is for you, then I would strongly suggest connecting to your guides and angels for assistance, as you will need to build a very strong relationship and bond with them in your rescue work. You need to become a team. I could never perform the work that I do without the assistance of my guides and angels. Many mediums in training for rescue work find that they experience spirits trying to step in as false guides. These spirits will act like a friend or advisor for you. They will try to influence you to make certain decisions that may or may not be in your best interest. Unsuspecting mediums will trust these spirits to be their guides and may not listen to their actual guides. These false guides may feel much stronger and come around more often. They may fill your mind with thoughts of power and greed, feeding into your ego. If you start using your gifts for your own gain and popularity, then you may be influenced by false guides. Your true guides will always want you to feel special, but they mostly emphasize using your gifts to help others. Your ego and social status should never be the motivating factor in your work.

It's best to make a strong bond with your guides. Each guide comes in with a certain vibration, so become familiar with their vibration and/or color. This will help your connection to them. As my guides always say, listen to your head, but follow your heart. Your guides should express their guidance and support through love and these messages will be felt through your heart. Spirits will communicate through your crown chakra or head. Always remember the difference.

The first step with any type of spirit work is through training and development. In order to become a rescue medium, you need to build and strengthen your skills in psychic development and mediumship. Search out and find a psychic or spiritual center in your area for classes, workshops, or individual sessions. Some teachers also have Web classes if you do not have centers in your area. Research and study as much as you can while developing your own unique style of psychic skills. Everyone is different and special in their own way. Some people can be stronger in clairaudience, whereas others are stronger in clairsentience, for example. You won't truly know what your strengths are until you start training. Circle groups are a great way to start practicing your mediumship as well. You can find circle groups that specialize in spirit rescue. This is the indirect technique that helps the spirit through remote viewing. Working together as a team will help build and strengthen your connection to earthbound spirits.

For the most part, mediums that were meant to work in spirit rescue will get the gentle nudge from their guides and angels that this type of work is something for them to look into. You may get drawn into the field by interest in the paranormal, near death experiences, or life after death. You may also get overwhelming attention from earthbound spirits, as they will be attracted to your special vibration. Those who are born to be rescue mediums will usually find that they attract heavier or denser energy around them as this type of vibration is best suited to work with earthbound spirits. As I've mentioned, the best way to tell if you have earthbound spirits around you is by their energy. Spirits that have already made their transition and have come by from time to time will feel much lighter when they communicate. Imagine this to be like a feather, blowing around in the wind that you sense around you. You know it's there, but it feels soft, light, and loving. For spirits that are earthbound, the vibrational level of their energy will seem more like a tumble weed rolling across the street and smacking you in the face. The connection will be heavy and intense. Spirits that are earthbound will attempt to connect to rescue mediums as often as they can if they are ready for help. If you come across this type of energy often, then you are probably a medium that can specialize in rescue work.

Though rescue mediums do specialize in lower vibrations, we also connect with higher vibrations when we connect to spirits on the other side. As my guides always say, it's best to work both sides of the field to maintain a proper balance. My years in rescue work have proven that connecting to the higher vibrations from time to time is extremely necessary as rescue work can become very heavy and difficult to handle over long periods of time. I find more often than not, those rescue mediums that do not raise their vibration periodically find themselves more susceptible to spirit attack. Your defenses can become compromised when you work heavily with earthbound spirits. It can be tiring with time because you're constantly trying to use psychic protection and defense techniques. This can be draining for most mediums. It's best to cleanse yourself, walk away, heal, and regroup. Working with higher vibrational spirits can help you feel energized as they send you positive vibrations and love. This is a great way to charge up your energy, like a battery. Once you feel stronger and clear from negativity, you can continue on with your rescue work.

Those who are interested in rescue work should be aware that your emotional state is equally important during training while working with spirits. People who have depression or psychological disorders, are in abusive relationships, or find themselves emotionally unstable should refrain from working as rescue mediums. Having a level mind and strong will is essential. If you feel you do not have thick skin or find yourself emotionally compromised, it's best you think about staying away from rescue work until you gain more emotional confidence. Most earthbound spirits are in need of aid, but the spirits with negative intentions can manipulate your emotions if you are not careful.

The best way to learn rescue work is by training with other rescue mediums. Because rescue work is only done by a select few, you may need to reach out and find rescue mediums through chat groups, online resources, or by referrals from a local psychic center. I do not encourage anyone to start working in spirit rescue without the aid of another trained and qualified rescue medium. Rescue techniques and psychic protection should be the main focus of your training. It may take months or years to fully understand the world of the earthbound spirit. Try to be of assistance, but maintain your distance from any negative spirits until you are properly trained. Search out and find rescue mediums with a good reputation. It's hard to determine if someone is a true rescue medium or only thinks that they are. There are many fake mediums out there preaching their gifts and experiences. Some mediums have an inflated ego and this will sometimes get in the way.

The best way to find the right medium to work with is to go with your gut instincts. Your intuition should be like radar, on at all times. Listen to what your gut is telling you; this is usually your guides and angels communicating with you. Your guides and spiritual advisors will try to help you find the right teacher. Another way you can tell if you've found the right rescue medium to work with is because they inspire you to learn and grow. Fake mediums are mostly looking to fluff their feathers and prove how strong a medium they are. If the medium only wants to talk about themselves and does all the work, then walk away. The focus of working with another medium is to learn. Listening to their stories and experiences most of the time isn't going to get you experience. Find an educated and supportive medium to guide you.

Though becoming a rescue medium is challenging, it's also one of the most rewarding types of mediumship. Not only do we get to connect with loved ones on the other side, but we also get the experience of helping spirits continue on with their journey by aiding in the transition. The love and compassion that you encounter through this transition is one of the greatest experiences you will ever have.

# 15
# Lessons

Spirit rescue serves many different purposes. Rescue mediums find themselves counseling spirits, aiding in a spirit's transition, clearing away residual energy, removing spirit attachments, and providing messages to loved ones from spirits. One main purpose of rescue mediumship that sometimes gets forgotten, but happens to be one of my favorite purposes, is the lesson learned from the spirit. I believe lessons that we learn from these earthbound spirits can serve to help the living who are suffering through hardships of their own. With every experience, there is a lesson to be learned that can be passed on.

What has the spirit learned and what can we learn from the spirit? Many people today are walking around experiencing the same exact problems that these spirits faced, like loss of loved ones, regret, failure, drug addiction, suicidal thoughts, addictive behavior, or depression.

I've always loved the saying, "A wise man learns from his mistakes; a wiser man learns from others' mistakes." I find it's best to learn from the experiences of others along with our own to help us learn and grow. The truth is no one really makes any mistakes. Mistakes or challenges that we face are lessons that help pave the way on our path called life. Without them, we wouldn't learn the valuable information for our soul's progression. I can't imagine anyone in this world living a perfect life. Everyone has experienced some sort of loss or failure. It's not the event that changes us; it's our reaction to it that makes the impact.

## Fear of failure

Regret and failure are two major emotions that everyone experiences. Most of us never live out the life we had intended due to fear or disbelief in ourselves. Sometimes our dreams or goals get pushed aside because of the requirements of daily life. These dreams never get fulfilled and therefore at the time of death, the individual finds herself regretting the choices that she has made. Could she have done more or could she have become more? How many times have you looked back at your life and thought about all the things you wish you could have done? What really keeps us from fulfilling our desires? Is it fear of failure or fear of the unknown? If it's fear of failure, then fear no more, because if you're not living the life you always wanted, then you have already failed. Every day you resist the urge to fulfill your dreams and desires, you fail yourself. As they always say, you will never succeed until you try. If you never try, then you will always fail. And if you've already failed, then what is left to fear?

## Fear of the unknown

Fear of the unknown is by far the strongest of all fears. If we don't know what is going to happen, then how do we anticipate winning or succeeding through it? Well, no one really knows what's going to happen in your life. I don't know anyone who has their whole life written down or planned out in front of them. You live your life everyday with a fear of the unknown. But why exactly do we fear this? Is it really so bad to not know what's going to happen? Couldn't we be excited with anticipation or hopeful instead? Instead of fearing what may or may not happen, go out and create it. It isn't until we try that we know what we are capable of and what could be created. So instead of fear, be full of hope. Hope is the shining light that guides our hearts to our desires. Follow it and it will never let you down.

# Regret

Spirits often look back on their lives wishing they could have said how much they loved someone or that they were sorry they didn't do more to express their love. The tragedy is that most people find this out once it's become too late. Through death, they find themselves regretting this and therefore hold onto the people they've lost. Is there someone that you need to express love to? Have you told your family and friends how much you care about them? We have to really look into the reasons why people wait so long to express their love to the people they care about the most. Is it because they feel there's no need? Do we anticipate rejection when we do so? Are we too busy? All seem to be logical answers, but none seem to be logical enough to fail in this task.

Expressing love to one another is one of the most important things we will ever do in our lives. There are those who believe success in their careers or material objects define their happiness. I find more often that at death, they find out it's the people that touched their heart that created the most impact in their life. Love is what makes your life worth living. People that you come to love will indeed make your life more fulfilling. Don't wait until death to realize this. Don't let fear hold you back. Tell the people you care about how much you love them every day. You may not get the same in return. They may not be able to express their love to you, but you don't love someone to get love in return. That isn't the purpose of love. Love is to give, express, and embrace. It isn't until you love someone unconditionally that you truly understand this.

## Letting things go

A great many spirits I've encountered expressed concern over things they couldn't let go. Their failures, regrets, mistakes, loss of loved ones, and obsessions were hard to release; therefore, they held onto these issues even after death. These issues created an emotional block to their happiness. If they weren't happy, then they weren't ready to move on.

Every day we find ourselves holding onto the things that keep us from happiness. These emotions are like weights, holding us down from continuing on our path. In order to find joy in your life, you need to let go of the issues you hold onto. Insecurities, obsessions, fear, pain, anger, loss, and even honor will hold you back. If you have control over these situations, then try to do something about them. Take charge and finalize these issues once and for all. Who wants to hold on to these issues all their life? If there is something that has been weighing you down that you have no control over, let it go! Holding onto something you have no control over will only hurt you. It's not productive and will never give you the result you're looking for. Once we're able to let go of the situations we have no control over, we can have time to work on issues we do have control over. Let it go and find your true happiness. Let the universe bring it to you!

## Mental illness

I've come into contact with large numbers of spirits that have experienced mental illness. I've also had the experience of living with and knowing people with mental illness, depression, or addictive behavior. It certainly isn't anything they felt they could control. Maybe through medications or counseling they can experience some level of comfort, but the symptoms are always there waiting to come out. For those who live with someone with a mental illness, life can be a struggle every day. Caretakers suffer just as much as the person they have come to comfort and care for. It takes strength and courage to succeed in this challenge. Spirits on the other side wish more often than not that they tried harder to control their symptoms. Unfortunately, mental illness in some cases is very hard to control. Connecting to each other, standing strong with each other, and loving each other can help overcome some of these burdens. Only through faith and hope can they find the light at the end of the tunnel.

Though spirits have many lessons to teach us, it's the lesson that means the most to you that helps you through life's challenges. I can only hope that the messages we receive from spirits can help us live more fulfilling lives. Life is too short to live with regrets, fear of failure, holding onto issues, and anxiety or depression. We need to rise above our challenges and create the life we've always desired.

I've asked my guides through the years about the purpose of our lives. Often, people face death questioning if they did all that they could and loved all that they could. What makes us truly know if our lives were successful? My guides tell me that it depends on how you view your life. When looking back on your life, the experiences you've had, the people you've loved, and the things you've accomplished, ask yourself, "Am I proud?" Are you proud of your life? Are you proud of who you've become and what you've done?

So I ask you, are you proud? Are you proud of who you've become, what you've done, and who you have grown to love? If not, then what do you need to do so that you are?

Life isn't easy and it's never going to be perfect. All we can do is our best. We may struggle, fall, get up, and fall again. Your life is defined by how you have pulled yourself up, not how you fell. Life is a lesson in the long journey of our soul. Allow yourself to fail and allow yourself to succeed. Be true to who you are and how you feel. Accept yourself, faults and all.

Life is a gift that one day will come to an end. Death is not an end result. It is only a process of change from one form to another. Our lives continue on and our love for one another will last forever. Do not fear life and do not fear death. They are one and the same.

So when it comes time for you to make your transition, follow your heart. Your heart is your guiding light to your family and friends, waiting to take you home.

# Conclusion

My hope is that the information I've shared in this book inspires others to view the world of the earthbound spirit in a more positive and thoughtful light. The cycle of life and death is an experience we will all one day share, and if this book changes your outlook on life and the afterlife, I believe I've done my job. Our perceptions of the world of spirits are constantly evolving, so that our fear, misconceptions, and doubt are replaced with faith, education, and understanding. Every day we encounter new possibilities; new ways to better understand our communication with the other side.

We've all enjoyed a good ghost story, a spooky haunted house, and a scary movie, but it's time to distinguish the difference between fiction and reality. There will always be negative spirits, just as there will always be negative people in the world. We can't control the negativity of spirits, but we can learn how to protect ourselves and control our own environment if we should encounter one. It's a big world and the spirit world is even bigger. Learn how to control your space and the energy around you.

You don't have to be a medium to have a strong relationship with spirits. They are around us all the time, watching over us. Some decide to keep to themselves, whereas others still long for a relationship and connection to the physical world. If you wish for a better connection to spirits, research psychic centers, circle groups, development classes, or chat groups to learn more about mediumship. Allow yourself to build a connection with spirits, angels, and guides to help you through life's challenges. Ask for protection from your spiritual protectors if you should ever feel threatened from spirits and connect to professional resources for assistance. You are never alone and help is always standing by to be of service.

Feel free to visit *www.amymajor.com* if you should have questions about rescue mediumship or if you are interested in training as a rescue medium. Everyone at times needs a helping hand, a shoulder to cry on, and a light in the dark. I'm always here to help. God bless.

# Glossary

**Affirmations:** Declarations or statements affirming that something is true.

**Angels:** Supernatural spirits or beings that protect and guide human beings.

**Animal spirits/guides:** Celestial beings in animal form that provide guidance and protection to humans.

**Apparition:** A visual appearance, often of a person or scene, generally experienced in a waking or hypnotic state.

**Astral plane of existence:** A plane of existence within the seven planes of existence, which resides in the spiritual world.

**Astral projection:** A result in which the astral body separates from the physical body.

**Attachment:** An act of attaching or the state of being attached by a spirit entity.

**Auditory spirit activity:** Auditory experience of a spirit, such as footsteps, bells, raps, and whispers.

**Aura:** A field of energy that surrounds all living things (people, animals, plants, etc.).

**Circle:** A group of people that sit around in a circle formation to communicate with spirits.

**Chakras:** Points in the body in which energy flows through.

**Clairaudience:** The ability to receive psychic information via hearing sounds or voices.

**Clairsentience:** The ability to receive psychic information through sensing or feeling/touching.

**Clairvoyance:** The ability to receive psychic information through seeing/visions.

**Clearing:** The act of removing energy from a person, place, or thing.

**Clearing specialist:** A specialist trained to clear away residual and spiritual energy.

**Collective apparition:** An apparition seen by more than one person.

**Consciousness:** The state of being awake or aware of one's surroundings.

**Crisis apparition:** An apparition in which a person is seen within a few hours of an important crisis such as death, accident, or sudden illness.

**Crossing over:** A common term to explain the full transition of a soul from the physical plane of existence to the astral plane of existence.

**Crystals:** Solid material constructed by Earth's elements which can be used for metaphysical properties to enhance and stimulate energy.

**Crystal grid:** A grid made up of protection and high vibrational crystals aligned in a geometric pattern to clear away and protect from negative energy.

**Death:** A state in which the physical and astral bodies separate completely.

**Demonic possession:** Possession by non-human negative entities or demons.

**Divine:** Of, from, or like God or a God.

**Dowsing rod:** A Y- or L-shaped rod that is sensitive to electromagnetic energy and spirit energy.

**Dream-like state:** A state of consciousness that appears to be dream-like or hallucinatory in nature.

**Earthbound spirit:** The soul/spirit of a person who has left their physical body through death and has failed to make the full transition to the other side.

**Emotional baggage:** Emotions that the spirit carries around with them.

**Energy:** A type of power or spiritual force, both positive and negative.

**Energy stimulation:** The change, removal, or addition to energy in a space by manipulating the vibration of the energy.

**Electronic voice phenomena (EVP):** Sounds found on electronic recordings that are interpreted as spirit voices that have been either unintentionally recorded or intentionally requested and recorded.

**Essential oils:** Concentrated liquid of aroma compounds from plants.

**Exorcism:** A religious or quasi-religious rite to drive out evil spirits.

**Free will:** A God-given gift to all humans that allows all people the right to make choices for themselves and have control over their actions.

**False guide:** A spirit pretending to be a spiritual guide.

**Ghost:** A popular term used to describe the spirit form of a deceased person.

**Gold Cord:** The connection between the Divine and an individual's soul.

**Gallery readings:** An event in which a medium provides spirit messages to a group of people in a gallery setting.

**Demonologist:** A specialist trained to release demonic energy from a person or place.

**Development circle:** A term used to describe a group of individuals that sit in a circle formation to develop their psychic, healing, and mediumship abilities.

**Direct rescue:** A spirit rescue technique that incorporates a direct communication link between the spirit and the medium.

**EMF detector:** A device used in ghost hunting for measuring electromagnetic fields.

**Ghost hunter:** A person who specializes in paranormal phenomena by investigating, analyzing, and evaluating data received in a paranormal investigation or ghost hunt.

**Guide:** A spiritual being in the spiritual plane of existence who assists in someone's personal life journey.

**Haunting:** A paranormal experience in which a spirit visitation is perceived by the physical world.

**Hypnotic state:** An altered mental state resembling sleep, but still felt by a level of awareness.

**Infrared camera:** A common device used in ghost hunting that forms an image using infrared radiation.

**Incense:** A material that releases aromatic fragrances when burned.

**Indirect rescue:** A spirit rescue technique that incorporates an indirect communication link between the spirit and the medium.

**Journeying:** A deep meditative state which allows the individual to go into an altered state of consciousness for spiritual communication.

**Lesson guides:** Spiritual guides that temporarily help the individual during challenges or lessons.

**Ley lines:** Natural fields of magnetic energy underneath the ground.

**Manipulate:** To control or influence energy.

**Meditation:** A practice in which a person can train their mind to create a state of consciousness for healing, guidance, or spiritual communication.

**Medium:** An individual with the ability to communicate with spirits.

**Mediumship:** The act of communication between a spirit and the medium.

**Message:** Information received by the medium from a spirit.

**Metamorphosis:** A paranormal term used to describe a shape-shifting ability.

**Mist:** A visual appearance from a spirit, mist-like in nature.

**Near-death experience (NDE):** An experience in which a person leaves their physical body for a short time and returns back without the conclusion of death.

**Ouija board:** A board with letters and numbers on which messages are spelled to form a communication between the physical world and the spirit world.

**Other side:** A commonly used term to describe the spiritual plane of existence or heaven.

**Paranormal:** A popular term used to describe something that is beyond the normal.

**Past life:** A past life is one that your spirit/soul has lived out before in another body.

**Past life regression:** A technique that incorporates hypnosis to recover or remember past life memories.

**Pendulum:** An object suspended by a thread to communicate with spirits.

**Pendulum grid:** A piece of paper marked with a circle and arrows to outline communication, such as yes, no, or maybe, between a person and a spirit.

**Physical medium:** A person who has the ability to manipulate physical manifestations from spirits.

**Physical plane of existence:** A plane of existence within the seven planes of existence, which resides in the physical world.

**Poltergeist:** A German word meaning "noisy or troublesome spirit." Poltergeist activity may include noises, objects moving, bodily harm, or feelings of being threatened. It's been thought that poltergeist activity is associated around people and not places.

**Possession:** When a person's physical body is taken over by an entity.

**Prayer:** An act by the individual to communicate to spiritual entities by reciting prayers, thoughts, or feelings.

**Psychic:** A person considered or claiming to have psychic powers.

**Psychic protection:** Techniques used to help stimulate the energy around a person, place, or thing to protect it against psychic or spiritual attack.

**Raps:** Knocking sounds associated with spirit activity.

**Reincarnation:** The belief that a person's soul is reborn into a new body after death from their current life.

**Remote viewing:** The ability to view a person or place from a distance through ESP.

**Reside:** To stay in or around a place of interest.

**Residual energy:** An imprint left behind during an event that resonates in an area over a given period of time.

**Séance:** A meeting that involves the communication of individuals and a spirit through a medium usually conducted through a meditative state.

**Sensory experience:** An experience in which an individual physically feels the energy of a spirit.

**Shamanism:** A spiritual practice that involves a person reaching an altered state of consciousness in order to connect to the spirit world.

**Silver Cord:** An individual's cord that connects the astral body to the physical body.

**Smudging:** The burning of incense or herbs to create a smoke-filled atmosphere to disperse residual or spirit energy. It neutralizes the energy in a person and place.

**Singing bowls:** Bowls made from crystal, metal, or glass that create sound vibrations.

**Spirit police:** Spiritual beings that oversee and enforce spiritual law within the planes of existence; protectors of free will.

**Soul:** The spiritual element of a person.

**Spirit:** The English word "spirit" comes from the Latin word *spiritus*, meaning "breath." It is the essence of all living things.

**Spiritualism (Spiritism):** Religious doctrines that advocate communication between the living and the spirits or souls of the departed through the act of mediumship.

**Spiritualist:** One who believes in the religion of Spiritualism.

**Spirit release specialist:** A specialist trained to clear away residual and spiritual energy.

**Spirit rescue:** A common term used for the communication, counsel, and guidance of earthbound spirits through a rescue medium to aid in their transition to the other side.

**Table tipping:** The act of communication with spirits through the use of a tipping table.

**Tipping table:** A round, three-legged table used during communication between the living and the souls of the departed.

**Transition:** The process or a period of changing from one state or condition to another.

**Vibration:** An instance of vibrating energy.

**Visualization:** A mental image perceived by a person.

**Visual spirit experience:** The experience of visually perceiving the spirit such as an apparition or aura.

**White light:** The light seen by those experiencing a near-death experience that is perceived to be a doorway to the spiritual plane of existence.

**White noise:** A hiss-like sound, formed by combining all audible frequencies.

# Resources

*Ghost Rescues: Working with Angels and Ghosts* (2009) by Sandra Staves.

*Spirit Rescue: A Simple Guide to Talking with Ghosts and Freeing Earthbound Souls* (2006) by Wilma Davidson.

*Ghosts and Earthbound Spirits: Recognize and Release the Spirits Trapped in This World* (2010) by Wilma Davidson.

*When Ghosts Speak: Understanding the World of Earthbound Spirits* (2009) by Mary Ann Winkowski.

*As Alive, So Dead: Investigating the Paranormal* (2011) by Mary Ann Winkowski.

*Spirit Rescue: A Dowser's Ghostly Encounters* (2006) by Tick Gaudreau and Dave Darrow.

*How to Remove Ghosts: Soul Rescue Manual for Incarnates, Spirits, Poltergeists, and Phantoms* (2013) by Bruce Darwill.

*Wayward Spirits and Earthbound Souls: True Tales of Ghostly Crossings* (2010) by Aniston V. Gogh.

*Journey of Souls: Case Studies of Life Between Lives* (2002) by Michael Newton.

*Spirit Release: A Practical Handbook* (2013) by Sue Allen.

*The Silver Cord or Life Here and Hereafter* (1946) by James Frederick and Olga Tildes.

*Jim Harold's Campfire: True Ghost Stories* (September 2011) by Jim Harold.

*Ghosts Among Us: Uncovering the Truth About the Other Side* (June 2009) by James Van Praagh.

*Unfinished Business: What the Dead Can Teach Us About Life* (May 2010) by James Van Praagh.

# Other great books by New Page Books

*Encyclopedia of Haunted Places: Ghostly Locales from Around the World* (September 2009) by Jeff Belanger.

*The Poltergeist Phenomenon: An In-depth Investigation Into Floating Beds, Smashing Glass, and Other Unexplained Disturbances* (January 2011) by Michael Clarkson.

*Encyclopedia of the Undead* (September 2011) by Dr. Bob Curran.

*The Lightworker's Source: An Enlightening Guide to Awaken the Power Within* (December 2012) by Sahvanna Arienta.

*Ghosts of War: Restless Spirits of Soldiers, Spies, and Saboteurs* (September 2006) by Jeff Belanger.

*The Power of Angels: Discover How to Connect, Communicate, and Heal With the Angels* (April 2014) by Joanne Brocas.

*Synchronicity: The Art of Coincidence, Choice, and Unlocking Your Mind* (February 2012) by Kirby Surprise.

*The World's Most Haunted House: The True Story of the Bridgeport Poltergeist on Lindley Street* (August 2014) by William J. Hall.

*This Book is From the Future: A Journey Through Portals, Relativity, Worm Holes, and Other Adventures in Time Travel* (July 2012) by Marie Jones and Larry Flaxman.

# Index

A

# About the Author

Amy Major is a psychic, empath, psychic medium, and rescue medium who has helped many people with her abilities. At a young age, she learned she had the ability to communicate with her spiritual and animal guides. Throughout her childhood, she developed astral projection as well as the ability to see auras and energy surrounding people. In her early 20s, Amy was told by her guides that she was able to communicate with spirits. While exploring her ability of mediumship, she quickly learned that she had very strong rescue mediumship skills. Amy now dedicates her time to rescue work and educating people about spirit rescue.

Amy has been a successful spirit rescue medium since 2002. She was a lead medium in the Psychic Ghostbusters Team through the New Millennium Psychic Center in Derry, New Hampshire. She works alongside other mediums and spirit rescue specialists to aid spirits in their transition to the "other side."

Amy has studied and worked at the New Millennium Psychic Center in Derry, New Hampshire for many years and is an active member of the Church of Spiritual Life in Methuen, Massachusetts. She is currently enrolled in Morris Pratt courses, specializing in mediumship and healing.